THE SALES PLAYBOOK

11 STRATEGIES
TO CLOSE MORE SALES

By David I. Hill

Published by Motivational Press, Inc.
1777 Aurora Road
Melbourne, Florida, 32935

www.MotivationalPress.com

Manufactured in the United States of America.

ISBN: 978-1-62865-286-4

CONTENTS

• • • • • • • • •

INTRODUCTION

· · · · · · · · · ·

I first realized the power of the phone when I was 12 years old. I grew up in some rough neighborhoods and was exposed to violence at a young age. When I would hear people screaming at each other and see fights break out, I knew it could escalate quickly, which wouldn't be good for anybody. Instead of helplessly standing by, I realized I could call 911 and the police would come to take care of the problem. Once they arrived, I felt safe and I knew my family was safe too.

While this wasn't the ideal way to start using the phone on a regular basis, it taught me the power it holds as a tool to connect strangers. I could pick up the phone, dial someone I didn't know who was in a location I had never been to, and spark a change in both of our days. To me, that was remarkable.

When I entered the working world, I never forgot the power of the phone. As a 17-year-old telemarketer, I felt a thrill when I could convince a potential customer to try our service, which seemed to happen to me much more often than my co-workers. I realized I had a unique talent that could be developed into something significant; something that would help me support myself and create the life I always wanted.

Over the past 28 years, I've mastered the art of selling on the phone. I've crushed my sales goals year after year in numerous industries, surpassing people who had much more experience and formal education than me. As I rose to the top in my last sales leadership role, I started using my knowledge to help thousands of salespeople hone their skills and make more sales. The results were astounding.

In this book, I share my best strategies, training exercises, and scripts, in the hopes of reaching even more salespeople. I guarantee this knowledge can change your life if you're committed to practicing and putting it into action.

CHAPTER 1

· · · · · · · · · ·

GETTING SMART WITH THE PHONE

"It's what you learn after you know it all that counts most."
John Wooden

It was early afternoon and I was walking to grab a salad for lunch when I noticed a text from a potential client. I had spent a good part of the morning with him and I personally thought we had an excellent meeting. I had expected him to get back to me with his signed contract, yet when I read his text message he was letting me know a competitor had just offered him a better rate. I quickly texted him back, asking if the competitor was offering the exact same resources and quality product. My goal was to show him how we were worth our fee, and if need be, make a counter offer before losing the business altogether. I kept walking, mentally preoccupied and impatiently waiting for his response. When I felt the phone vibrate I buried my head back into the conversation, eager to push for the close. I suddenly sensed something in front of me and BOOM. I saw a bright flash of light and stars.

When my vision returned, I realized I had walked head first into an aluminum telephone pole and almost knocked myself out. Not only did I have a serious bump on my head (and later a black eye), the pole jarred the phone out of my hand and it lay smashed on the ground. I picked up the shattered phone, considering myself lucky it didn't fall a few inches over into a sewer drain. At least with a broken phone, I had a chance of transferring my contacts to a new phone. I headed to the Sprint store immediately.

Three and a half hours and almost $500 later, I was finally able to reconnect with the prospect. He had just signed with my competitor.

When I think back to this situation, I wonder why I didn't just pick up the phone and call the prospect as soon as I got his text message. He probably would have answered my call and we could have talked right then. It was the perfect opportunity to adjust my presentation, given the new information I'd learned, and go for the close before he could reconnect with my competitor. That would have been the sensible thing for me to do. I know that now, after having the sense literally knocked into me by the pole.

On an episode of *The Tonight Show*, Jay Leno held up a smart phone and said, *"These phones are so smart you can do anything with them. The only thing we don't do with them is call people."*

There's a hidden goldmine in your pocket. You might think that shiny iPhone or Samsung Galaxy is worth a few hundred dollars, but what if I told you it could be worth thousands or even millions over a career? If you work in sales or own a business, your answer to propelling your career forward is to use your phone as a device to speak with and influence other human beings. Yes, your phone may be "smart" and allow you to send emails, tweets, texts, and selfies, but that doesn't mean those are the smartest ways to communicate with prospects.

Aside from meeting with people in person, talking on the phone is the best communication medium for contacting prospects because it enables personal connections. Instead of print on a screen, you become a real person on the phone. And so does your prospect. You can learn a wealth of information about people from just a short conversation and read between the lines of what they're saying in a way that most electronic communication does not allow. Since you're communicating in real time, you can adjust your questions and responses to fit their unique situation. In other words, the conversation becomes personal. (And you can keep your head up so aluminum poles don't sneak up on you.)

Everyone knows that sales is all about making connections. Many customers are more likely to buy from a sales rep when they feel a personal connection. The phone is the best tool for forming these connections, yet it's underutilized by the majority of salespeople today. That begs the important question: *Whatever happened to talking on the phone?*

Depending on your age, you may remember the days before the Internet, smartphones, or even cellphones. The days when a family shared one landline and an answering machine that stored everyone's not-so-private messages. Calling people and receiving calls, for yourself or someone else, was a common occurrence. After all, it was the fastest and most convenient way to communicate. It was how people kept in touch with friends and family, and managed things like scheduling doctor's appointments. People used the phone so often, it was common to have a library of numbers memorized for quicker dialing. Some of you may even remember the days having to wait for your brother, sister, mother or father to get off the phone so you could make plans with a friend. That has certainly changed.

With the advent of new technology, society has slowly shifted away from its use of the phone, at least in regard to leveraging it as a device to speak with other people. Instead, we have a variety of communication options such as email, text messages, Facebook, LinkedIn, Instagram,

Snapchat, GChat, and more. All of these options are certainly handy in various situations, but they've fundamentally changed society's norms for communicating. Instead of having two-way live dialogues, people are accustomed to sharing their thoughts in 140-character tweets, or giving others encouragement by simply clicking a "Like" button. While social media and electronic communication are great in a lot of ways, it's impractical to rely on these mediums too heavily. While we gain some advantages, we lose others. Because of the differences in age, behavior, interpretation, and a generational gap, many sales people today aren't sure how they should connect with a prospect. Or maybe more importantly, how they should *not* contact or try to connect with a prospect. Despite the recent decline of talking on the phone, it is still one of the best communication tools available for sales. You just have to know how to use it effectively.

THE TOOL YOU'VE BEEN MISSING

Becoming good at phone prospecting can open the door for what you've been wanting most out of your job. Whether it's more money, better job security, improved work/life balance, bragging rights, or just having more fun at work, all of these outcomes are a result of becoming more effective at your job. When you improve your phone prospecting skills, I am certain you will become more effective and make more sales. How can I be so sure? Because reaching your highest conversion rate is a result of employing the correct *combination* of communication methods. That's right, using multiple methods to contact prospects. (Don't worry—this book isn't about convincing you to delete your email address or social media accounts.) Just like email isn't the right way to contact prospects all of the time, neither is calling them. A variety of methods are ideal for the salesperson's playbook. Unfortunately, salespeople have a tendency to lean on the communication method they are most comfortable with like it's a crutch. Over time, it actually turns into a crutch, since skills for other mediums deteriorate as they go unexercised.

If you're like the vast majority of salespeople, your underutilized communication method is talking on the phone. Even when you know calling a prospect might be your best option in a certain situation, you don't always choose to pick up the phone, or you don't invest enough time in practicing calls, scripts, and role-play to do it well when it counts most. As such, you're missing opportunities all of the time. By improving your phone skills, you'll increase the likelihood of closing many more deals.

For example, you may need to send prospects detailed information about your services. Giving them this information in writing may be the best (or only) option to share it. In this case, contacting your prospect via email is a smart option. However, if you were also to call the prospect to let her know you were about to email her, highlighting the main points of your email to help her digest the information quicker, that might work even better. If you got her voicemail, you could simply leave a message.

Here's a play call example:

> » *"Hi Miss Clark! It's Brian Smith from ABC medical supplier. I just wanted to let you know I'm about to email you some information about our products. I wanted to be very thorough, but I know it can seem like a lot of information. To make things easy for you, the main points you'll want to consider are the one-page FAQ sheet and the chart that compares us to competitors. Please let me know if you have any questions. If I don't hear from you by next week, I'll go ahead and call you again to check in. Thank you! Again, this is Brian Smith and my number is XXX-XXX-XXXX."*

With this phone call, Brain has just made Miss Clark's job easier. If he hadn't made this call, Miss Clark could have easily skimmed his email, opened a long sales document, and felt overwhelmed by having to review so much information. However, with the accompanying call, she knows what to read to get the answers she wants most, and she knows it's OK to skip or skim the rest for now. How much more likely do you think she will be to take immediate action and review Brian's offer, rather than ignoring or deleting his email, or procrastinating her review? A lot more likely. And in this particular instance, Brian increased his chance of winning her business in less than two minutes, including the time to log the message in his tracker and take thorough notes in his Customer Relationship Management (CRM) system.

If this sounds like an incredibly simple way to close more deals, that's because it is. I've worked with thousands of salespeople over the course of my career, and I've seen how a little knowledge and practice using the phone can transform people's levels of success. This book will not only teach you how to make better calls, but when to make them.

A MORE STRATEGIC APPROACH

It's hard to be strategic about selling when you're having one-way conversations. It can also be a painstakingly slow process. However, when you get so used to doing things a certain way, your standards adjust and it's easy to "settle" for things that are less than ideal. When you switch to calling prospects more often, the first thing you're likely to notice is the change of pace in which you make progress, since you will be talking with more people.

For example, when you rely on email, social media, or even direct mail, you become used to waiting for a response. Although people can reply in an instant with electronic communication and you can have a back-and-forth conversation, this doesn't typically happen in sales. Many sales reps send out fairly generic messages to prospects, or even worse, an e-blast or mass mailing to multiple prospects. And then they wait to hear back from people. It's a reactive approach. When your professional success and income depend on people responding, this is an incredibly frustrating way to go about your business. Who wants to play a waiting game? With phone prospecting, it's a different story—a proactive approach. You reach out to people to connect with them live so you can gauge their interest in real time. The phone is also an excellent tool for qualifying leads. No matter the outcome, when people pick up the phone you get instant gratification. You're making progress. You're gaining knowledge you didn't have before, which will allow you to combat objections and help customers understand when you're selling something that could truly benefit them. You go for the immediate sale but if that doesn't work, you can at least gain a better understanding of what would need to happen to close them in the future.

As a play call example, if you're selling insurance, a lot of people already have policy and aren't actively looking to switch. If they get an email or letter from another provider, they are likely to ignore it. However, if they get a phone call, they might tell you they are covered. You could ask when their coverage is up, and they might tell you June. You could let them know you'll call back in early May when they're thinking about renewing. Alternately, you could invite them to send you a copy of their current policy, and say you'll do your best to give them a lower rate for the same or better coverage. You might also be able to find out what company they currently use so you can adjust your presentation accordingly. Whatever your approach to handling their objection, you are in a better place than you were before making the call. Why? Because you know what's keeping them from saying yes today, what competition you're up against, and when they are likely to consider your offer in the future.

Another play call example of when the phone can be used to support existing sales efforts is for sales reps who go business to business. I have spoken with some B to B reps who tell me, "I don't use the phone because we have to get in front of the decision makers." I get that, but my suggestion is calling ahead and doing some reconnaissance. Think about it. Before you jump in the car and head out, what information would help improve your chances of closing a deal? Call ahead and try to find those things out. For instance, you could ask who they use for the product or service you're selling. Many times, the receptionist has no issue telling you. You can also ask who the decision maker is, when he or she will be in, and maybe even get the opportunity to set an appointment. Yes, this type of call takes time, but often less time (and less gas) than showing up randomly trying to catch a busy decision maker whose name you may not even know. This example shows how supplementing existing efforts with calling prospects can help make your sales approach and presentation a little more strategic.

On the other hand, after speaking with prospects on the phone, you may learn they have zero interest in what you're selling and there's no point in reaching out to them ever again. (Or that they should go into a long-term email marketing/drip campaign because they are not interested at this time or may be committed to a competitor.) While that may sound like bad news, it's actually great news because you know not to put forth any more effort into winning their business. It's a lot harder to get that response from emailing or sending direct mail, since people who are uninterested in your services are also likely to be uninterested in your messages or flyers. Rather than emailing you back, they might ignore you, block your email address, or mark your messages as spam. Or they might toss all of your sales materials in the trash. None of these options are helpful for salespeople.

When you speak with people over the phone, it's quicker and easier to gauge their interest. While this is a benefit, sometimes salespeople think of it as the opposite because they are afraid to hear "no." More specifically, they are afraid to hear a forceful and irritated "no" with an accompanying "don't ever call me again," or "take me off your list."

Here's where I need to make something abundantly clear: a quick "no" is a gift, regardless of how it's packaged. Whether it's friendly or angry, a quick "no" is an opportunity to ask great questions and turn the no into a yes, or immediately move on to other opportunities. It's a chance to waste zero time trying to sell something to someone who will never buy it. Although it may seem hard to hear, it saves you valuable time and false hope. When you do the majority of your prospecting in a reactive way, such as email or direct mail, you will get fewer quick nos. While that may sound like a good thing, it's actually not. Nothing can suck the positive energy out of a salesperson more than continuing to do something over and over without generating a positive result. When you reach out to a lot of people and get very little response, it's easy to get discouraged. Furthermore, "good" lead lists can create unrealistic expectations. You may think you're making progress by spending time emailing people or sending LinkedIn messages and tracking how many times you've contacted them, but the people on your list may never read your messages or they might be totally uninterested. You probably feel productive by contacting so many leads, but you aren't vetting them to see if they're likely to convert into sales. If you have a huge lead list, you may even stop caring about qualifying prospects because you figure if you contact them enough times, you're bound to close some deals. This can easily turn into playing a numbers game you just aren't going to win because your efforts are misguided. In essence, you're doing "busywork," which is defined by tasks that keep you busy but have little value. Now, if you were on salary with zero commission and your boss assigned you busywork that would be one thing. But in a role where your livelihood depends on making sales, it's easy to see why doing busywork is self-defeating. Let's focus on purposeful work!

Although most salespeople would agree with this, it's astounding how hard it can be for people to transition out of doing this kind of work. Of course it can be difficult to break habits, but more importantly, people are hesitant to stop doing the tasks that seem the easiest. And sending a bunch of messages or postcards can certainly be easy. Many salespeople turn these activities on autopilot while hanging around the water cooler, posting on Facebook or chatting with co-workers and they don't realize they are actually wasting valuable time in the office. Even worse, some salespeople make it a habit to work from home while watching bad daytime television or texting friends while they "connect" with prospects. This type of work may lend itself to a perfectly pleasant afternoon—except for the fact that nothing was truly accomplished. If making sales matters to you, which I think it does since you picked up this book, you cannot continue to spend time on low-return activities.

Instead of contacting a prospect in a reactive way multiple times and tracking your outreach, you often save yourself that effort by picking up the phone. When you call prospects and take a proactive approach, you ramp up on your productivity. This may sound surprising, since many salespeople think using the phone is more time-consuming than sending electronic messages or snail mail, but it's the truth. If you're interested in making more money, increasing your productivity will give you additional time to reach out to other prospects and ultimately close more deals. If you're interested in better work/life balance, your increase in productivity will allow you more free time. Whatever your goals, calling prospects more often will help you succeed. While you may not get to zone out doing busywork, I'd be willing to bet making more money or having more free time would make it worth it.

You know what's even better than that? By transitioning to doing more prospecting over the phone, your interactions with potential customers will remind you of why you decided to go into sales in the first place. Chances are, you like meeting new people, building relationships, helping people and working to win people over. It's challenging to combat objections, but it's also exciting and fun, especially when you become really good at it. The fast-paced nature of the business puts your skills and knowledge to the test and keeps you on your toes. Maybe you feel a rush when customers see the value of your products/services and you close a deal. Or maybe you feel a deep sense of fulfillment when you are able to help a prospect. Whatever your motivation, to engage in this type of high-energy selling, you simply have to communicate with prospects in real time. When you avoid calling people on the phone, you're not only bowing out of the most efficient and effective type of selling, you're decreasing your chances of experiencing the aspects of sales you find most gratifying.

PLAY BOX EXERCISES: INSPIRE, CONFIDENCE, EFFECTIVENESS (ICE)

I have included play box exercises throughout this book to help inspire you, build your confidence, and help you become more effective. I promise these exercises work, but only if you do them! Each one should only take a few minutes, but the return you will get is well worth the time investment. You should write your answers down in a notebook or the space provided in the book. You can also go to www.davidihill.com and download a free worksheet with all of the questions. Remember, do not continue reading until you complete each play box exercise!

PLAY BOX EXERCISE: WHAT ARE YOU HOPING TO ACHIEVE FROM IMPROVING YOUR SKILLS ON THE PHONE?

In 2009, I was on a mission to have a better work-life balance. I was burnt out from working too many hours and it was making me bitter about a job I used to love. I wanted to reduce my stress level and spend more time with my family, so in 2010 I hired my first business coach. With his help I adopted a better pre-qualification process to increase my efficiency. It worked. That year I made almost the same income as I did in 2009, but I only worked about 60 percent of my usual hours. It was liberating. Even better, I grew to like my job again, and that helped me feel reenergized both at work and outside the office.

Maybe you can relate to my situation a few years ago, or maybe you have totally different goals or aspirations. Whatever the answer, complete the following exercise before you continue reading.

Take five minutes and write down the results you're hoping to achieve by reading this book, whether it's more money, time, or both.

What would you do right away if you could increase your income by 25 percent but work the same hours? Would you buy a new car or take the family on a tropical vacation? What if you suddenly had a few extra hours each day? What would you do? Would you teach, write a book, or do that volunteer work you've always thought about doing? Who would you spend the extra time with if you made the same money in 60 percent of the time you are working now?

_____

_____

_____

_____

_____

_____

_____

_____

_____

KEY TAKEAWAYS

Using the phone to talk with prospects will help you:

» Be more strategic: Learn more about prospects and better tailor your communication

» Increase productivity: Know which leads to pursue and manage your time better

» Reinforce why you went into sales: Helping more people and closing more deals feels good

With all Play Box Exercises in this book, **do not move to next chapter until you complete them.**

CHAPTER 2

. . . .

CONNECT OR BE DISCONNECTED

*"Things turn out best for the people who make the best of the way
things turn out."*

John Wooden, They Call Me Coach

As a salesperson, you're not only selling products or services, you're selling YOU. Customers are buying the experience of working with you as an individual. Your positive attitude, sparkling personality, trustworthy demeanor, or however else you present yourself. Why? Because in order to buy something, customers have to interact with you to some degree. The more they like you, the more pleasant the experience will probably be for them and the more willing they are to go through the buying process with you instead of someone else.

Using the phone will give you an advantage in bringing your personality front and center. When done well, you can make an instant connection with prospects. When done poorly, you'll hear a click.

In this chapter, we'll focus on how you can learn a wealth of information about prospects just by hearing their voice, and how to better connect with prospects through conversation.

MASTERING THE FIRST IMPRESSION

Research has shown that people only have seven seconds to make a first impression.[1] In that short amount of time, you can be perceived positively or negatively, and it's hard to switch camps after that. That's why the first few seconds of a conversation with a prospect are vital in establishing a good connection.

When meeting in person, it can be hard to gauge whether you're making a good first impression, since people won't usually turn and walk away from you abruptly if they aren't satisfied after seven seconds. But it's a different story on the phone. People can hang up without feeling overly guilty or awkward, and you won't even have a chance of redeeming yourself after a bad first impression. (Remember, prospects aren't sitting around waiting for your call. Usually they are in the middle of something else and a sales call is a distraction.) On the phone, your first impression can make or break you. But don't let that scare you! The phone gives you the golden opportunity to make a first impression, and that's valuable in itself. When you contact prospects with just email or direct mail, you may not make an impression at all. No impression means no sale.

MIRROR AND MATCH

Although people can appreciate a wide variety of personalities, it's usually easiest to bond with others who are similar to you. Think about your group of friends, and even the co-workers you would consider as your friends. You probably have quite a bit in common with them, right? Maybe you're laid back and so are they. Or maybe you all have a sense of humor and you like to joke around together. Maybe you share a love for playing golf, traveling, or watching *Game of Thrones*. These similarities in personality, demeanor, and interests strengthen your bond and make it fun to spend time together. Of course you're probably also friends with people who are different from you, but it might have taken longer to build those relationships. For example, if you're a very direct person who always says what's on his mind, co-workers who value sensitivity and acceptance might find you a little rough around the edges. On the flip side, you might find yourself impatient with those same co-workers, believing them to be over-sensitive. That isn't to say you all couldn't become the best of friends, but you see how it might be a rockier road to get there.

The same is true in sales. The best way to gain rapport with prospects is to be like them. Don't get me wrong here—I'm not saying you should become someone you're not. I'm simply saying you should adjust your approach depending on whom you're talking to. Chances are, you do this already. The conversation you have with your buddies is probably not the same conversation you'd have with your 80-year-old neighbor. That doesn't mean you're being insincere when you speak with your neighbor or your buddies. You're just magnifying certain aspects of your personality and choosing to discuss topics that your audience could relate to. Why? Because you want to have pleasant interactions. This is the same approach you should take on the phone with prospects. The challenge is homing in on your prospects' personalities and interests when you've never met them before, and getting good enough at it to very quickly build rapport. About seven seconds quickly. Luckily, there are a variety of cues you can look for that will help you mirror and match:

Pace: The rate or pace in which people speak says a lot about their personality and mood. A slower pace could show prospects aren't in a hurry, or they have a laid back attitude. It could also tell you they are analytical and listening to all the details. A faster pace could show a no-nonsense direct and to-the-point personality, or that someone is in a rush. Age and geographic region also influence how quickly people talk. Adjusting your pace to mirror your prospects' will not only make it easier for people to process what you're saying, but make it less likely they'll feel overwhelmed or annoyed while conversing with you.

Mood: If your prospect is in a bad mood, you shouldn't try to mirror it. But in other cases, it's helpful to show you're on the same level. When prospects are enthusiastic and friendly, you should kick those emotions up a notch. When prospects joke around a little, you can joke around too and use it as an opportunity to build even more rapport by laughing at their jokes, even if they aren't that funny. If prospects are sarcastic, you can be tastefully sarcastic too.

Language: Using similar language sends a message that you are like the other person; that you have similar perspectives and possibly a similar background. Whether or not this is true, it makes people feel comfortable talking to you and opening up. If prospects are formal or casual on the phone, it's best to follow their lead. If they mention certain goals or concerns, take note of the words they used so that you can refer back to them in the same way.

Greeting: One of the easiest ways to mirror prospects is by matching their answer to the question, "How are you?" This is such a simple opportunity to build rapport but salespeople frequently miss it. If you want to immediately establish a bond that you are like the other person, you won't be successful if you openly start out on a different level. For example, if your prospect says she's doing "Oh, pretty good" and you reply that you're doing "Excellent! Happy to be alive on this beautiful day!" how do you think she is going to feel? Alienated! Probably like she wants to get off the phone with you. I know a guy who whenever you ask him how he is doing he says, "I am unbelievable!!!" One time he said, "If I was any better there would have to be two of me!!" People find it so annoying that they avoid talking with him. He thinks he is just being positive but as you can see, he is taking it too far.

AVOIDING COMMON PITFALLS

Saying certain things will stop your conversation before it even gets started.

Mispronouncing Names: Having a lead list with names can be helpful, except when you aren't sure how to pronounce the names. A difficult-to-pronounce name creates a conundrum for salespeople because using names is a good way to make conversations feel more personal and build relationships. As Dale Carnegie famously said, "The sweetest sound to a person is their name." When you say a prospect's name wrong, it's a dead giveaway that you don't really know the person you're calling. This is a red flag for a gatekeeper to deny you access to the decision-maker. If you're speaking with the decision-maker already, it's a reminder that she doesn't owe you the time of day—you can't even say her name right! If you are not 100 percent sure of pronunciation, it's best to ask for clarification. People typically don't have a problem with this, since it shows you care. It can also create a bit more rapport than mispronouncing a name. Alternately, if you have a first and last name on your lead list and you think you can pronounce one of them correctly, go with that. However, you should only use "Mr." and "Ms." if you know the prospect's gender. That brings me to my next point.

Assuming Gender: One of the best ways to make a good first impression is by being polite. That's why I always address prospects as Sir or Ma'am. Unfortunately, this backfired on me one time. I was doing a B to C call and I didn't have the name of the prospect. The person who picked up the phone had a deep voice, so I said, "Hello Sir. How are you today?" Clearly offended, she yelled, "I am not a Sir!" Click! There was no recovery from that one. I knew I wasn't selling the lady anything.

I'll be honest. This mistake threw me off of my game a little bit because it affected my script. I always use Sir or Ma'am, and suddenly I felt like I couldn't say it with confidence anymore. After a bunch of calls I was able to shake the greeting anxiety, but my best advice is not to guess on gender. Right before I addressed this lady as Sir, I realized I wasn't 100 percent sure of her gender. But I decided to take a guess. And now I highly recommend *not* guessing on gender. If there is any question, then the best greeting is a simple and friendly, "Hello!"

The Greeting One-Up: Another thing to watch for is the phrasing in your greeting. You probably know that the grammatically correct way to say how you're doing is "well" rather than "good." In sales, however, making prospects feel *good* is more important than grammar. My friend is particularly attuned to this after a memorable experience she had with a high school teacher. In her waitressing job, my friend noticed how customers reacted when they said they were doing "good" and then she said she was doing "well": like she was pointing out their bad grammar and talking down to them. Wanting to make better tips, she became conscious of potentially offending customers by one-upping them, and she got in the habit of saying she was doing "good" even though she knew it was grammatically incorrect.

Her teacher had the opposite approach. She would stand in the hallway and ask students how they were doing as they walked into her class. My friend would say, "I'm good thanks. How are you?" And her teacher would respond, "I'm doing WELL," making a big point about the word choice. While the teacher might have had good grammar, what my friend remembers most is how the interactions made her feel.

That's what your prospects will remember about you too—how you made them feel. If you want to relate with other people, don't be clueless about your greeting.

IDENTIFYING PERSONALITY AND BEHAVIOR TYPES

There are a wide variety of personal assessments out there, and you may be familiar with some of them, such as the Myers-Briggs, the DISC, and Gallup's Strengths Finder. In fact, many organizations make personality and behavior assessments a required part of the hiring process or a mandatory part of 360 performance reviews. It may feel like these employers are trying to uncover your deepest darkest flaws, because in a way, they are. Personal assessments are surprisingly effective in understanding how people think and why they behave the way they do. While people can be conscious of their behavior and adapt it to fit various situations, personality is hardwired and typically doesn't change over time. Certain personality types typically mesh together nicely whereas others clash and are almost destined to struggle with seeing eye-to-eye. This is because personality type is a major indicator in how people approach getting things done.

As an example, let's use the DISC assessment. Personally, I am a fan of this assessment and I have all of my salespeople take it before I hire them. The DISC is based off of four behavioral traits. While the interpretation and description of these traits vary depending on the DISC provider, I typically use an assessment that acknowledges the following: dominance, influence, steady/stable, and compliance. Each of these DISC traits is measured on a low to high scale depending how questions are answered. In almost all cases, people will have one trait that is highest, which can be considered a general description of their behavior. Here is a quick look into each one:

» D: direct, results-oriented, forceful, driven, and self-confident

» I: social, enthusiastic, persuasive, lively, and emotional

» S: team player, accommodating, patient, consistent, and understanding

» C: detail-oriented, analytical, exact, reserved, and careful

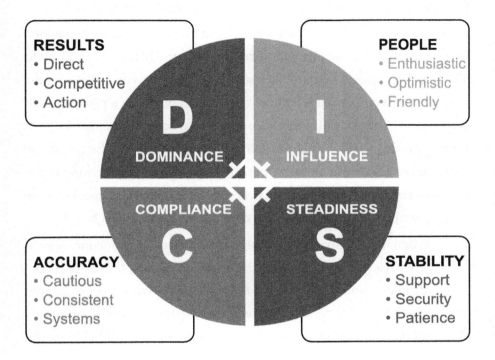

Based on people's DISC results, I gain a much better understanding how to communicate with, relate to, and engage them. While the results are helpful to have, most of the time, I can predict the outcome before people even take the assessment. Chances are, you could guess which DISC trait is the highest for you without even taking the assessment.

But the interesting thing here isn't just assessing your own behavior; it's understanding how other people are different from you and how they will perceive your behavior. For example, if you score highest in I—Influence, aka High I, you are on the high end of the spectrum when it comes to being persuasive and social. (I use this as an example because many salespeople are High Is.) When talking to a prospect who is a High C or High S, your enthusiasm may come across as being overconfident, aggressive, or conceited. When talking to a High D, your social approach might seem inefficient and annoying. All of these perceptions can damage your chances of connecting with prospects and ultimately closing.

As you can see, the challenge is predicting prospects' behavioral preferences and tailoring your presentation to their preferred style. This can be difficult at first, but it gets much easier with practice. I am to the point where I can tell almost immediately where a prospect falls on the DISC scale within a few seconds of conversation. Being a High D, I am naturally direct, but because of my understanding of behavior and awareness I am able to tailor my presentation for other behavioral types. Don't worry, with awareness and practice you can do the same. Here are some examples of how I adjust my communication approach:

» When I find myself speaking with a High S, someone who is sensitive and dislikes change, I'm not going to push as hard as I normally would. I know that I'm speaking with a good listener who isn't going to get impatient and rush me off of the phone. I can take it slower and build a connection through being polite, sincere, and showing I am trustworthy.

» When speaking with a High I, someone who is social and enthusiastic, mirroring those traits and relating on a personal level matters most. This is where I would try my hardest to find a common bond or interest, and build rapport around that.

» With a detail-oriented High C, I know I need to be organized. My presentation would include lower-level details than with other types because High Cs do their research and they want quantifiable facts and data. I would also make a greater effort to take copious notes, including direct quotes, and repeat them back later to show I was listening.

» When I find myself speaking with another High D, someone who is decisive and impatient, I know I need to get to the point quickly without beating around the bush. High Ds will consider what I'm saying, but when they get it, they ultimately just want to move on to the next thing and do it quickly.

It's important to recognize that some people are naturally relationship-oriented (I and S) and others are task-oriented (D and C). This affects how they view the world and the way they go about getting things done. Along the same lines, some people are action-oriented (D and I) and some people are reflection-oriented (C and S). As a salesperson, knowing how people are hardwired will help you tailor your presentation so that it resonates with them. Should you push for the sale or back off? Should you focus on building a social connection or stick to the facts of your product or service? When you know what behavior type you're talking to, you'll have a better idea of what to do.

I encourage you to read more about personality and behavior types to gain a better understanding of how to relate to different types of people. Honestly, adjusting my style to different types of people was something I learned the hard way. For years and years, I lost business from High Cs because I was underprepared. The first time this was brought to my attention was years ago when someone I highly respect administered a high level assessment on me, and he told me I focused more on selling optimism and assurance than facts and data, which some people need. Sometimes the truth hurts but without the awareness we can't make the changes needed to get to the next level. Your best option for increasing your self-awareness is to take an assessment, since they often give specific instructions on how, given your results, you can communicate and work more effectively with others. If your company hasn't offered free assessments yet, talk to your manager or HR leader. Otherwise, you can find a variety of assessments for free online. Once you learn your personality or behavior type, you'll be able to access even more information on relating better to different types of people. (Some assessment types like the Myers-Briggs even have a sort-of cult following where you can connect with other people who have the same personality type. Those groups can be just for fun or helpful for improving your professional skills.) Trust me, the better you get at connecting quickly with various personalities the smoother your prospecting calls will go.

BE INTERESTING

If it were as simple as it sounds, we would all be the most popular person at the party. The guest people crowd around to be entertained. Wouldn't that be nice to experience, both in social situations and in sales? Well, the best way to capture people's attention and hold it in the palm of your hand—whether at a party or on a prospecting call—is to be interesting. Just because you're selling something people might actually want and need doesn't mean they will listen to you long enough to discover your value to them. You have to draw them into conversation by piquing their interest. In truth, some people are naturally better conversationalists than others. Luckily, practice and hard work can make up for any shortcomings. Here are some tips to be even more interesting than you already are:

Intonation: Remember your monotone science teacher that put everyone to sleep? You don't want to sound like him on the phone. If you sound like you're bored with your sales presentation, you can bet your prospects will also be bored. But unlike your science teacher, your prospects have no obligation to listen to you. Try making a greater effort to raise and lower the pitch of your voice. An exaggerated example is how you would read a storybook to a child. Yep, the same strategy works for keeping adults entertained.

Vary Your Pace: We already talked about choosing a good pace overall for talking, but it's smart to have some variation in there to add interest. When you get to the most important points, slow down a bit to let the information sink in. You can also try a longer pause after you say something powerful, where you wait an extra beat for emphasis. Don't feel compelled to fill a conversation with words when your prospect may need a moment to think and process what you've just said.

You Know the Trick Phrase: You know what makes people's ears perk right up and listen? A question like the one I just asked you. When you say something along the lines of, "You know what's really interesting?" or "You know what's most surprising?" or "You know why that's so different?" it draws people in. They sense you are about to get right to the point and tell them what they want to know. It also has a similar feeling to thinking you might get called on in class. (Quick. Focus. I might need to say something.) It's a great trick for highlighting certain aspects of your presentation.

The Active Mmm Hmmm...: One of my favorites. A major part of your conversations should be spent listening, which we will get into in another chapter. You may think it's hard to be interesting when you aren't talking, but that isn't the case. You need to make sure you aren't giving your prospects the feeling like they are talking to dead air. To be an active listener, throw in some sounds or interjections like "wow!" "really?" "no kidding!" or "Mmm Hmmm!" that show you're still there and interested in the conversation. If you're taking notes at the same time, this might feel like rubbing your stomach and patting your head at the same time. It's hard, but it's worth it.

Use Stories: A big part of sales is educating potential customers on their options. Unfortunately, sharing that information can sometimes seem a little dull, especially when it comes to a plethora of facts and details. How do you keep it interesting? Try adapting some of the information in your sales presentation to a story format. Instead of just talking about a certain feature, try telling a story about how a customer used that feature to transform their business. In a longer format, this would be called a case study, but you can insert mini versions into conversation pretty easily. It's also a great way to show how many happy customers you've worked with.

SUMMARY

The more you use the tips in this chapter, the more you'll experience the advantage of using the phone to connect with prospects and the power of two-way conversations. If you were primarily emailing prospects in the past, you'll gain the advantage of better tailoring your presentations to match your prospects' personalities. You might have sent out messages, texts, or direct mail pieces in the past and wondered why people weren't responding. After speaking with more prospects on the phone directly, you'll understand why. Some people must have thought your messages were too long, or too formal, or too casual, or too impersonal, or too boring. Or maybe you just got lost in the shuffle of all the electronic messages and paper mail they receive. By picking up the phone, you learn a wealth of information about prospects in just a few seconds. By hearing a person's voice, you get a good read on personality and demeanor, and it's easy to understand motivation.

A major benefit of calling prospects is the ability to better prequalify your leads, which will make you more efficient and increase your win rate. Instead of meeting with people in person who aren't very motivated to buy, you can prioritize your opportunities and spend time with the people you are most likely to close. We will get into this more in Chapter 5, but know that this is a key benefit of connecting through two-way conversation.

While talking on the phone may be on the decline overall, the number of people who own a cellphone has risen dramatically to 92%.[2]

Since email has become so widespread, calling prospects can actually be an incredibly effective method for cutting through the noise of your competitors. You gain the advantage of standing out by doing something different. You get your prospect's attention. And while you have it, you can show your personality and likability. Being polite, friendly, relatable, knowledgeable, and trustworthy will put you in the best position to gain prospects' business. Although people won't always buy from you, calling them on the phone and building a real connection will give you the best opportunity to close more sales.

KEY TAKEAWAYS

» Master your first impression: The first seven seconds are crucial

» Mirror and match prospects: Pace, mood, and language

» Identify personality types: Tailor your presentation to the prospect's personality

CHAPTER 3

· · · · · · · · · ·

LIFTING THE 800 LB. PHONE

"Get comfortable with being uncomfortable."

Anonymous

Now that you understand why the phone is such a valuable sales tool, all you have to do is pick it up! Unfortunately, sometimes that is not as easy as it sounds. Even if you start out eager to use the phone, your enthusiasm may fade after continually hearing no. It happens to the best of us. I call this state of mind (and state of hesitant action) "call reluctance." People experience many forms of call reluctance, but they all lead to the same result: neglecting to make your sales calls or making fewer calls than you should to garner the best results.

In my twenties I started working for my family's business, which was a magazine for professionals in the condo management industry. My job was to sell advertising space. I thought I had conquered the nervousness I felt when I first started making cold calls in my prior sales jobs. Having a few "difficult" sales roles under my belt, I considered myself a veteran on the phone. But as both my new boss Kristin and my mom pointed out to me one day, I wasn't making very many sales. Actually, I hadn't made any new sales at all—just a few renewals that they gave me. At the time, this didn't concern me much. My mom was the boss and I felt un-fireable. Also, a manager had never held me accountable for making a certain number of sales, so it wasn't something I focused on. In past positions I did my job of picking up the phone and *trying to* make sales, and that was that. I had relative success but magazine ads were a different product and Kristin was a different boss. She said sales is about the numbers, and I knew she wasn't too happy with my numbers thus far.

One day Kristin suggested we make calls together the next morning and I had no choice but to agree. I knew she wanted to understand what I was doing that was resulting in zero sales that weren't renewals. Immediately, I felt a wave of anxiety. Would she think I was a bad salesperson and that I had no business working there anymore?

The next day I was sitting at my desk when I heard Kristin come in. I wish I could say that I stepped up to the plate and made good on my promise to make calls with her, but I didn't. I hid under my desk and waited for her to leave. After I was sure she was gone, I snuck discretely from the office, ashamed of my behavior. I called her later apologizing for not coming in that morning, saying I was out on the road visiting a few leads in person. She said it was fine, but of course she wanted to reschedule our plans to call prospects together.

In the moment of hiding under my desk, it felt like I could make my call reluctance go away if I just ignored it awhile. But of course that didn't work. I realized that if I wanted to continue working at my family's company and working as a salesperson in general, I couldn't be afraid of talking to people.

I share this story because I know a lot of people can relate to it, whether or not they want to admit it. Maybe you've never hidden under your desk to avoid calling prospects, but there are likely other ways you've exhibited call reluctance, maybe without even realizing it. If you find yourself focusing on organizing paperwork, researching your leads, tidying up your desk, or answering low-priority emails instead of picking up the phone, you are likely procrastinating because you have call reluctance. If you can relate, you're definitely not alone. In any situation, people are frequently inclined to put the hard stuff off for later, and calling prospects can be hard.

There are several different root causes of call reluctance. Determining which type you're dealing with is the first step toward getting past it.

» Fear of Rejection

» Lack of Role Acceptance

» Not Knowing what to Say

» Over-Analysis

» Fear of Success

I'll share a quick summary of each type of call reluctance and then we'll go directly into the solutions.

Fear of Rejection: Hands down, this is one of the biggest problems salespeople face and the top reason they are hesitant to pick up the phone. This type of call reluctance tends to create the most anxiety around cold calls! Talking to someone on the phone creates more of a connection than other communication mediums, but it can also make rejection *seem* more personal. The word here is *seem* because rejection in sales shouldn't feel personal. You could be the best salesperson in the entire world and you still wouldn't win them all. Some prospects will always say no and some will always be grumpy when you contact them. It can be hard to separate yourself emotionally from harsh responses, but it's essential that you do.

Lack of Role Acceptance: It's hard to deny that salespeople some-times get a bad rap. Whether it's being overly aggressive and hounding customers to buy or not having customers' best interests at heart, a few bad apples have spoiled some customers' impression of sales. Not to mention that plays and movies like *Glengarry Glen Ross* often serve as reinforcement of negative stereotypes.[3] Even when salespeople want to help customers, sometimes they feel uncomfortable selling their product, service or themselves. My good friend and business coach John Alexandrov brought this form of call reluctance to my attention. Through coaching hundreds of salespeople he says this type of call reluctance holds a lot of people back, and it can be easy to overlook.[4]

Not Knowing what to Say: This is a big one because it is so closely tied to confidence. If you aren't sure how to answer questions or respond to objections, of course you're going to be a little nervous to pick up the phone. Even if you're sales veteran, this form of call reluctance can reappear whenever you start selling a new product or service, or if your manager wants you to adjust your presentation to highlight different selling points.

Over-Analysis: Some people are prone to over-thinking things. Unfortunately, when you analyze every possible scenario, especially what could go wrong, you're likely to psyche yourself out. The longer you prepare for a single call, the fewer calls you'll end up making and the less you'll get done. It's important to become so comfortable with calling prospects that you don't need to over-analyze it. Some salespeople who aren't over-analyzers by nature can become that way as a form of procrastination. It's important to watch out for this unhealthy behavior and stop it early on.

Fear of Success: This cause of call reluctance might seem strange, but it's real. When you do something differently, like make more sales, things change. Your win rate, commission, and your place in the pack all change as you become a sales leader. That can be scary for several reasons. First off, you might have to keep calling people because it's working so well, and that might not be something you think you want to do. You also set the bar higher for yourself and supervisors or sales managers may expect you to operate at the higher standard, which can be hard work. You might also be frustrated with yourself for spending months or years missing out on getting the results you could have had if you picked up the phone sooner. Success seems clear-cut, but as you can see, it's often complicated.

PLAY BOX EXERCISE: IDENTIFY YOUR SOURCE OF CALL RELUCTANCE

After hiding under my desk, I did some soul-searching and realized my source of call reluctance was that I was unsure what to say. I hadn't worked at the company very long and I wasn't yet accustomed to the most common objections. I didn't feel that confident in my knowledge and that made me feel less confident in my delivery. As a result, I felt shy about my boss listening to me speak with prospects.

Did any of the sources of call reluctance feel familiar to you right away? If so, write it down in the space below. If you could relate to multiple sources, include them all.

_____

_____

_____

_____

_____

Over the next week or two, keep a journal next to you as you make calls. Before each call, jot down what's on your mind before you pick up the phone. This will help you uncover any other causes of call reluctance you might not have realized were holding you back. Before you move on any further, go get yourself a journal or notebook. Seriously, do it now! This is going to make a huge difference. You don't have to marry the idea of keeping a journal - just date it for a few weeks and see how it feels.

Great job getting your writing tools. And now let's get to the good stuff: the solutions for conquering all forms of call reluctance! I'm going to present a ton of great options in this chapter and it's up to you to find what works best for you as an individual. Chances are, all of these solutions will be helpful, but one or two will absolutely change your life. As I go through the solutions, I'll explain which ones are typically most effective for the different types of call reluctance.

MINDSET

One of my favorite stories on mindset comes from my friend, personal development coach and author Jairek Robbins. In his book *Live It*, Jairek talks about how he was working for his grandpa's lumberyard in college and hating every minute of it.[5] Not only was it hard manual labor, it was incredibly monotonous and boring. The tasks were repetitive, carrying and stacking lumber to and from the same piles over and over, and none of Jairek's co-workers spoke English so he couldn't talk to anyone all day. Jairek took the summer job to show his dad that he could learn the meaning of hard work through personal experience. If he made it through the summer, his dad agreed to let him enroll in Semester at Sea, something Jairek badly wanted. But after a few miserable weeks, Jairek wondered if he could stand going to work every day to fulfill his end of the bargain. That's when he started thinking about what needed to change if he wanted any chance at success: his *mindset*.

Instead of letting negativity cloud his thoughts, Jairek made a point to start noticing the good things about the job. First off, the scenery was beautiful working out in the woods. The air was fresh, the temperature was cool and comfortable, and it was usually sunny. Second, the job was basically a built-in opportunity to work out. All of the heavy lifting was making Jairek stronger, and by focusing on the fitness aspect, the repetition felt more productive. Third, Jairek realized the silence around him was a blessing because he could get headphones and listen to whatever he wanted. He invested in audiobooks and was no longer bored by the monotony of his job.

By making the decision that he was going to enjoy work, Jairek changed his reality. He found the good in what he was doing and focused on it until it overpowered the bad.

I love this story because it illustrates the power of mindset. The reality is that no job will ever be perfect. There will always be certain tasks that you would rather not do or certain aspects that are a source of annoyance. But it's up to you whether you focus on the negative things or the positive. Don't get me wrong—changing your mindset isn't as easy as flipping a switch. Some people are naturally blessed with a glass-is-half-full mindset and others have to work harder to see the world through a positive lens. Wherever you're currently at with your mindset, know that it's possible to improve.

There are a variety of strategies in this book that will help you keep a positive mindset, but one of the most effective strategies for me is to remember to have fun. Yes, I'm doing my job, but that doesn't mean I can't have fun at the same time. Whenever I notice that I'm starting to take myself too seriously or that I'm letting a grumpy response from a prospect affect my mood, I remember to smile, laugh, or make a goofy face at myself in the mirror. In fact, I keep a mirror in front of my desk just for this purpose. It may sound silly and that's because it is. Work should be fun. Life is too short to walk around in a bad mood all the time.

PLAY BOX EXERCISE: COUNT THE WAYS YOUR GLASS IS HALF-FULL

What do you like about your job? Maybe it's that every day is different and you always get to meet new people. Maybe you feel great because deep down you know you are really helping people when they buy from you. Or the flexibility in your schedule allows you to watch your kid's soccer games. Or maybe you've become great friends with your co-workers. Whatever you like about your job, no matter how small, write it down in the space below. Better yet, write it down in your journal or notebook, or on a piece of paper you can tuck in your desk drawer. Whenever your mindset needs a pick-me-up, read the list of reasons you love your job.

_____

_____

_____

_____

_____

Improving your mindset will help you get a better perspective on what really matters. This transformation is most effective for conquering fear of rejection and over-analysis because you'll start to realize it's not such a big deal when prospects shut you down. When someone hangs up on you, the world doesn't come to a grinding halt. You're still the same person you were 30 seconds before. Your family and friends still love you, the sun is still shining outside, and you can still go to your kid's soccer game. Those few seconds of rejection were barely a blip on the radar. When you start to really believe rejection isn't as painful as you once thought, any tendency for over-analyzing calls should fade away. Each time you pick up the phone it will feel like no big deal. You won't have any reason to over-analyze what may or may not happen on the call, and you'll be able to crank out more calls than ever before.

FIND YOUR WHY

Simon Sinek wrote a powerful book called *Start With Why*. I first read it years ago and his words have stuck with me for a long time and helped me stay motivated while calling prospects. Sinek says we all have different reasons why we do the things we do. For example, why do you get up and go to work every morning? The most obvious answer is to get a paycheck. We all need to have money to live. But is it really the money that motivates you?

For me, it isn't about the money itself—it's about providing an amazing life for my two daughters, Jaquilyn and Samara, and also for my wife, Vee. I want my daughters to have the things I didn't have growing up. Thinking about all of the great things I could provide for them inspires me to work hard every day. This is my *Why*. Instead of thinking about the "what" every day, which could get me down, I focus on the Why. This simple strategy helps me concentrate on the big picture instead of the outcome of individual calls. I know that every call I make is supporting my Why, regardless of whether it ends with a close.

Remembering your Why can be especially helpful for overcoming any type of call reluctance because your Why trumps any reason you might not want to pick up the phone.

So how do you keep your Why top of mind? I always encourage salespeople to create a vision board. A vision board is a collection of your goals, dreams, and desires, all represented in a collage. You might already be familiar with this concept, since it's one aspect of the personal development world that was quick to go mainstream, thanks to the book *The Secret*. A vision board serves a few purposes. First, it's based on the law of attraction, which is the idea that focusing on certain things in life can manifest those experiences. (i.e., if you focus on positivity, especially certain positive outcomes, you will bring them into your life.) While this is a widely debated topic, the second purpose of the vision board is hard to deny: it's motivating to be reminded of all of the things you want in life. For example, my vision board contains photos of my daughters and wife, which reminds me of how much I want to create an amazing life for them. It also has a photo of a tropical scene, reminding me of the vacations I can afford to take with my wife when I work hard, and a photo of a BMW racecar I will buy someday, and my amazing view from our patio overlooking the ocean from our oceanfront home. When creating your vision board, you definitely want to include your Why, but you should also include a bunch of other things that will get you excited and help motivate you. You can use magazine clippings, photos, or anything else for that matter. Just make sure you post it somewhere visible. If you're on the road a lot, tuck it in a notebook to keep with you or make a smaller version you can keep clipped to your car's visor.

I actually put motivating images in multiple places so I'm reminded of my goals throughout the day. I put motivational notes to myself on my bathroom mirror so it's the first thing I see in the morning and the last thing I see before bed. The home screen on my phone is a photo of a '69 Chevelle because my dream is to restore one. My family and I are in the process of buying a new home with a larger garage, partially so I can pursue my car restoration dream. Seeing the photo of the Chevelle multiple times a day has kept me focused on it and I'm getting closer to making the dream a reality. It is also making my wife happy because she wants a larger home closer to her family. Do you see how the *what* is the house, but the *why* is the restoration of my dream car (for me) and larger home closer to family (for Vee)?

Whenever you start to feel discouraged during the workday or when you're at home, look at your motivational images and refocus on your Why. Keep those images in mind before you make your next calls.

KNOW YOUR NUMBERS

What ultimately helped me the most to get past my call reluctance was what Kristin and other sales leaders said from the beginning: sales is a numbers game. Not just in reaching monetary sales goals, but in contacting enough prospects that you speak with enough people who will say yes. Because no matter how good you are at sales, some people will always say no. In fact, a lot of people will say no.

Now, depending on the product or service you're selling, the average number of nos for each yes can vary. You might hear no 20 times before you hear yes, or maybe even 50 or a 100 times. It also depends on the leads you're calling. When I worked for the magazine sometimes I would call the companies that placed ads in the phone book. Since these are pretty much the "coldest" calls a salesperson can make, I could hear 200 nos before I got a yes. When I called past clients or referrals, the numbers were usually much more in my favor. Follow-ups from a tradeshow also yielded a little better results. So depending on the source of your leads, the numbers change. Whatever the average number, it's important to know it and keep it top of mind. Why? Because for every no you hear, you are one person closer to hearing yes.

I've heard Tony Robbins advise salespeople to break down their average commission from one sale into the total number of calls they typically need to close one deal. For example, if you average $300 in commission for one win and it takes about 30 calls to close one deal, each time you call a new person it's like making $10. In essence, you can thank people for saying no and walk away each time thinking, "I just earned $10."[6] This is a much better mindset than "poor me!" This mentality helps me remember that even though I'm hearing no over and over, I'm making progress and getting closer to my goal. When number 17 says no, I don't worry about it because I know that statistically, he wasn't supposed to say yes.

PLAY BOX EXERCISE: KNOW YOUR NUMBERS

When coaching new clients the first thing I have them do every week is send me three numbers: how many contacts they made, how many appointments they went on and how many sales they closed from the appointments. In the beginning, those are the only numbers I am concerned with. The numbers create clarity. If salespeople are making a lot of contacts but they are not leading to appointments we know they have to work on scripts and dialogue. If they are setting appointments but not making sales we know to work on conversion. The numbers do not lie.

To be able to coach you in this book, we need to get a better understanding of your numbers as well. Do you know the average number of calls you have to make to close one sale? If you've been logging your calls, go back and review your progress to calculate an average number. Write it down here. _____ If you haven't been logging your calls, it's time to start. In the next chapter we'll go over best practices for logging calls, but for now, you should at least make note of every call you make, the type of lead, where the lead came from, whether it turned into an appointment, and whether you were able close it into a sale. You can download a free template on my website (www.davidihill.com) to track this information.

UNDERSTANDING YOUR VALUE PROPOSITION... AND ARTICULATING IT

Why do customers buy what you're selling? It's a simple question, but getting to the answer can be harder than it seems. If you're sometimes reluctant to make calls because you aren't sure what to say, working on your value proposition will make a big difference. When you fully understand your value proposition and you can clearly articulate it, you will know what to say to prospects in any situation. Your confidence will shine through in your voice and you'll take your phone prospecting skills up a huge notch.

Most salespeople have a decent grasp of the top selling points of their products or services. Usually, this information is given to reps upfront during training, and often through trial and error, they learn which selling points are most attractive to prospects in various situations.

However, there are probably a lot of reasons why someone might buy what you're selling, and the more you know about your product or service, your industry, and your competition, the more selling points you can come up with. This is definitely a positive thing, but sometimes the myriad of selling points can bog you down and cloud your value proposition. To make it even more complicated, your value proposition isn't static; it changes over time as the industry evolves and your competitors change. Luckily, there are several things you can do to home in on your value proposition:

» **Ask current customers why they value your product or service.** This tip is simple but surprisingly rare. If you handle renewals as well as new business, it will be easy to ask current customers the next time you speak with them. If not, you might have to do some digging. Companies often gather customer feedback through surveys but don't think to share it with salespeople. If you aren't sure if your company has this information on file, ask your manager. Your company may need to start obtaining customer feedback or remove interdepartmental information silos so salespeople can access that feedback.

» **Talk with your co-workers about your interpretation of the value proposition.** Even if everyone has the same company training, nuances in how salespeople communicate the value proposition can be eye-opening. It's a great idea to have meetings to discuss the value proposition as a team. If calling that type of meeting is out of your span of control, you can always ask your co-workers individually.

» **Do a focus group.** Get a bunch of your customers together in person or on a call and ask them to talk about why they value working with you. Better yet, ask non-customers why they don't work with you, and what would need to change for them to become your customers. This is a great way to see your company and value proposition from a new perspective.

» **Keep it simple.** People are bombarded with information nowadays, and anything you can do to simplify your messaging will make it more effective. If you feel like your value proposition bogs you down, your prospects will feel the same way. To simplify, try separating the main benefits from ancillary benefits. Lead with the most important points and save the rest for later, if needed.

» **Start with Why.** Sinek has the right idea about motivation and you can tap into his advice in your value proposition as well. Customers connect with a company's mission and values—*why* they do things—more than *how* they do them.

» **Don't go on autopilot.** Even if you think you know your value proposition like the back of your hand, it can become outdated quickly with just a small change in the industry or a new offering from a competitor. Try any of the aforementioned tips for checks and balances purposes.

These tips might seem like extra work, but it's worth it. Your call reluctance will fade when you fully understand your value proposition and it will be much easier to refine your messaging.

COMING FROM A POINT OF CONTRIBUTION

If your call reluctance stems from a lack of acceptance in your role, listen up! This will probably be the most helpful strategy for lifting your 800-Lb phone. Sometimes salespeople procrastinate in calling prospects because they feel like they're bothering them. These salespeople make up all kinds of reasons why they shouldn't pick up the phone:

» "I think she was just being nice when she told me to check back with her in a month."

» "I've already left him one voicemail and I'm sure he would have called back if he were interested."

» "I don't want to call...
  » too early"
  » too late"
  » and interrupt lunch"
  » and interrupt dinner"
  » on Mondays because people are usually busy"
  » on Fridays because people sometimes go out of town"
  » etc.!

What do all of these thoughts have in common? In each case, the salesperson assumed that not bothering the prospect was more valuable than the benefits the prospect could stand to gain from buying the product or service. Let's think about that for a minute. If the best way you think you can help a prospect is by *not* contacting them, you must not think very highly of whatever you're selling. Either that, or you don't think very highly of your ability to actually help people.

I interviewed a person named Jessie who struggled a lot with accepting her sales role. When she graduated college, she got a sales job at a furniture company and everything about the position seemed foreign to her. Instead of feeling proud of her new job, Jessie said she felt awkward and embarrassed. She was uncomfortable reaching out to people she didn't know and she worried constantly about being too pushy or annoying. This mindset put her in a place where she wasn't happy in her professional life. But one day, she finally got sick of feeling that way, and she thought, "Screw it! What do I have to lose by interrupting people?" Jessie realized her job was to give customers the option of working with her and it was OK if they said no. She started placing a higher value on herself and stopped thinking she was a "lowly person asking powerful people for help." When Jessie experienced that potential customers appreciated her support and she started building real relationships in the industry, it all came together for her. That was eight years ago and she's still at the same company.[7]

As a salesperson, your job is to educate potential customers on how your products or services could help them. After all, that's why people buy things; they need or want them for whatever reason. Salespeople help customers understand their options so they can make the best decisions for their unique situations. My mentor, Chairman of the Board at Keller Williams Reality International, Gary Keller, says he always thought about his role as an information-giver and it helped him become extremely successful in sales.[8] He never thought about sales as trying to convince people into buying things. Instead, he has always viewed the sales role as informative and educational. This changed how he felt about calling prospects. Instead of feeling like a nuisance, Keller believes that prospects are just waiting for him to call. He feels an obligation to contact prospects and share accurate information to help them, especially before the wrong person shares information that could lead to a bad decision.

This mindset is a little like a personal value proposition. Keller knows he will provide a good sales experience by being honest, ethical, and fair with prospects. He also knows that unfortunately, not all salespeople provide that type of experience. Keller focuses on helping prospects instead of closing them, and that's something he can feel good about. If you can get into the same mindset of coming from a point of contribution—I mean really have it coming out of your pores—your job will become much easier. You'll see your role as genuinely helping people, and your fear or anxiety about making calls will disappear.

Another great thing about this mindset is that you'll become less attached to closing each sale. Sometimes it can be easy to get wrapped up in making your numbers or that rush you get from closing a deal. Instead of thinking about the individual prospect and being present in the moment, salespeople sometimes check out of the process and focus only on the outcome. But being a *good* salesperson is about more than just selling. When you do your job of informing prospects of their options, they may choose to not buy from you. And that's OK.

Along my journey as a salesperson, I had to learn how it's much better to be committed to helping people rather than committed to the outcome of closing the sale. When I was working in real estate when I was younger, I had a tendency to push prospects to take the offers on their homes that *I* thought were good offers. I made it about myself, and assumed that everyone else should think like me. I genuinely believed that what would be a good deal to me should be a good deal to them too. But this way of thinking didn't serve me well. When I would get pushy with prospects, they would either fire me or take the deal and be left with a less than favorable impression of working with me. Even if they got what they wanted, they didn't like the feeling of being pressured or rushed into a decision. Those customers never gave me referrals, which I realized showed they weren't satisfied with my work. I was surprised to learn that ending in a close doesn't automatically make all sales a positive outcome. Instead of pushing for the sale, win, commission, or however you want to think about it, it's better to let people make their own decisions without any additional unwarranted pressure. Yes, you can be assertive (especially in time-sensitive situations) and encourage prospects to make decisions, but you need to know when enough is enough and you are no longer being helpful. (We will cover this topic in more detail later in the book.)

Having this mindset saves me a lot of frustration when I don't close a deal. When I've spent a lot of time talking with a prospect and he ultimately chooses not to work with me, I don't see it as a waste. Why? Because my goal was to come from a point of contribution and help him make a decision—not to convince him into buying what I'm selling. In other words, I'm committed to helping him, but I'm not attached to the outcome or idea of him buying from me. So as long as I've done a good job presenting my value proposition and sharing accurate information, it doesn't feel like I've been rejected.

CHAPTER SUMMARY

While the phone is a great tool for connecting with prospects, it's different from what you might be used to. It could take time and hard work to build your confidence and skills, but don't get discouraged! I promise you that focusing on the key points of this chapter will lighten the weight of the 800-Lb phone, which will feel like weight lifted off of your shoulders.

———

KEY TAKEAWAYS

» Mindset: Your thoughts become your reality. You are in control of your thoughts.

» Numbers: You won't win them all and you don't need to.

» Contribute: Your job is to provide information that helps people make their own decisions.

Additional Resource:

If you want to learn more about call reluctance, I recommend reading *The Psychology of Sales Call Reluctance: Earning What You're Worth in Sales* by George W. Dudley.

CHAPTER 4

· · · · · · · · · ·

GET SYSTEMATIZED OR GET LOST

"I value self-discipline, but creating systems that make it next to impossible to misbehave is more reliable than self-control."

Tim Ferriss

I will always remember an instance when I was working in the publishing business and I called on a national account. I had managed to get the decision maker on the phone and he told me that my timing was pretty good because they were having a meeting to discuss next year's advertising budget in about 45 days. He told me to follow up in 30 days and he would let me know what he needed from me. I was super excited and remember writing this information down somewhere and getting back into my calls.

About two months later I saw the company's ad in a competitor's magazine. I called the prospect back right away. He remembered me and asked me why I never followed up after our initial call. All I could say was that I was sorry but I forgot. Clearly my response did not cut it. Being forgetful or unorganized aren't qualities people typically look for when deciding what companies to work with.

What went wrong here? It wasn't that I forgot to follow up. It was that I didn't have a good system in place for taking notes and tracking my future to-do items. If I did, that prospect should have been an easy close. From that point on I made a commitment to myself that any time I had a promising conversation I would properly log it and set a call back appointment. You could say this single lost sale was my defining moment for becoming systemized!

In this chapter, we'll cover the basic systems all salespeople should have in place to set themselves up for success.

A SYSTEM FOR TAKING NOTES

When you use the phone for prospecting, you have a lot of direct touch points where you connect one-on-one with another person. Although those conversations will mean something to you at the time, after a full day of making calls, they will probably become a little hazy. A week later, you might not remember any of the details. A month later, prospects' names might not seem familiar at all.

Instead of feeling overwhelmed by the number of people you're connecting with and all of the details of their situations, you should plan on forgetting it all. That's right. Don't even try committing that stuff to memory. Why? Because your brain works hard enough already and unless people sometimes compare you to Rain Man, tracking the details of your sales calls as mental notes probably won't work out for you. There are other aspects of prospecting that will need to be committed to memory, such as scripts, so I recommend you save room for those things instead of details about individual calls.

That said, you need to track the details from your calls somehow or you won't have a clue what's going on with your prospects. Who's ready to buy soon and who still needs time to think? Who were you joking with about Fantasy Football, and which lady went to your alma matter?

It was all so clear last week... and then you went on living your life. Your only chance of retaining the information you learn from calls is to write everything down.

In case you skimmed over that last part, I'll repeat. Write. Everything. Down. You never know what details might be important later, even if they seem trivial now. Every aspect of a conversation can help you learn about your prospect and enable you to better tailor your sales presentation. There have been countless times that I ended up closing a sale because I took great notes from a past call. I'll reference things from my notes that I don't even remember because the conversations happened so long ago. And you know what? It works. If there is only one thing you take from this book, it should be how important it is to set yourself up for a good follow-up call. If you're dedicated to taking great notes, you'll have a huge advantage when it comes to closing. You'll know how your product or service can help your prospects, so you'll know what angle to take in your presentations. By referencing past discussions you will show you paid attention and that you are organized. You will also create rapport. Sometimes, it's these little things that make the biggest difference.

I recently called a new prospect for the first time and he said he couldn't talk to me right then because he was dropping his son off at college. I told him congratulations and asked what college, and I took a note that he said UMass Amherst. When I called him back the next week I asked how the ride to UMass Amherst went and whether his son was getting settled in. Right off the bat, I was able to make a good connection on the second call because I took good notes. (I also asked a good question, which we'll get into in a later chapter.) And yes, I closed the sale.

The best thing about taking notes is that you can do it however you want, as long as you follow one condition: develop a system that works for you and use it for all of your calls.

We haven't talked much about speed, but it's an important part of sales. The more people you talk to, the better your chances of closing. The quicker you are at taking good notes, the more calls you can make.

Paper or Digital: This is the first thing to consider. If you have a CRM system, you definitely want to save your notes digitally. However, even if you don't have a CRM system, I still strongly advise saving notes digitally. It's just a smarter way to organize information and ensure you can access it quickly when needed. As an example, I was calling a prospect from a new lead list we purchased, and I suddenly realized I was speaking with someone I'd connected with months before. She remembered who I was and for a few seconds I felt like a deer in headlights because I couldn't remember a thing about her, aside from the fact that at one point I knew who she was. Luckily, I was in front of my computer and I looked up her name in our system, allowing me immediate access to my notes from our last call. If I had only used paper and pencil to save my notes, how long would it have taken me to find her information? Considering how many calls I make, I might still be looking for it. Even without a CRM system, saving notes in Word or Excel will allow you to search the document for specific words later and find what you're looking for.

But what if you're a slow typist? If you peck-peck-peck at your keyboard with your pointer fingers, you probably won't be able to take notes fast enough to capture all of the details. In that case, you should take notes on paper the old-fashioned way. Just know that this is only the first step in your process, since you still have to convert your paper notes to digital. It may seem like you're doing double the work since you're taking notes twice, but it's honestly not a bad system. (Maybe I'm biased, because this is my system.) When I type up my notes, it gives me an opportunity to reflect on the call and add anything I might not have recorded initially. What I do is take bullet points and piece the story together when I add to my CRM.

I could work on my typing skills with the goal of taking notes digitally, but frankly, I don't want to. I am a notebook and sticky note kind of guy. I surround myself with writing utensils and places to jot down notes because I like to get up and move around when I'm calling prospects. I do a better job on the phone when I can be mobile, and typing doesn't really mesh with that. My system is to write things down on the closest notebook and add my notes to the CRM system later. When I use a dialer, sometimes it's easiest for me to take shorter notes on my computer after each call, but it took a lot of practice for me to get to that point. (We'll talk about dialers in another chapter.) Some people would consider taking notes on paper an old-school approach to sales but if it works for you, don't feel pressured to change it.

Individually or in Groups: You can either save and finalize your notes after each individual call, or wait until you've made many calls and save all the notes in one swoop. There are pluses and minuses to both options, and it really comes down to whatever works best for you.

If you type your notes during calls, it might be easiest to finalize and save them as you go. You can quickly add any comments and details and move onto the next call. If you write your notes by hand, it's going to take you a little longer to convert them to digital. Some people like to do it right away while the conversation is fresh in their mind. It also helps avoid a notes-conversion session later, which isn't always the most exciting part of the day. On the other hand, some people don't like finalizing notes after each individual call because they feel like they lose momentum for future calls. If you mentally psyche yourself up for cold-calling, stopping to work on notes after each call can feel inefficient because you're constantly switching gears. My best advice is that if something feels disruptive to your productivity, it probably is.

You should decide whether it works best for you to finalize and save your notes after each call or after a bunch of calls. If you prefer to save them in chunks, just make sure you don't wait too long. The more time that passes after you speak with someone, the more the memory of the call will fade and the quality of your recall will decrease.

WHAT TO NOTE FOR EVERY CALL

In addition to taking copious notes on your calls in general, there are certain things you should specify about every single call you make. Before you skim over this section because it seems like basic information, know that there's a great chance you aren't taking the level of notes you could be taking, and that changing this single aspect could make a huge impact on your numbers. I have experienced over and over again how often my notes help me bring in new business, especially during the follow-up process when I hardly remember talking to people. Do yourself a favor here, and really read this list. It will vary slightly depending on your company and industry, but it's an excellent starting point.

The person you spoke with: This seems like a no-brainer, but it can be easy to forget in the moment, especially if you didn't speak with the person on your call list. Did you speak with the decision maker or a gatekeeper? Did you learn any new names? Write it down.

Motivation: Is the prospect ready to buy ASAP or does he need some time to think? It's important to assess this and make note of it because it will affect your follow-up plans. It's common to label prospects' motivation levels as A, B or C, or Hot, Warm, and Cold, respectively. A/Hot prospects are motivated to buy now. B/Warm prospects are interested, but don't plan on buying for maybe another month or two. C/Cold prospects could be motivated to buy in the long term, but not anytime soon. (C prospects often include people who are locked into contracts.)

Personal details: Recording personal details that prospects just happen to mention can help you later. Like with my prospect who dropped his son off at UMass Amherst, you can bring these details up later to show you were paying close attention and that you care about your customers.

Commonalities: Similar to personal details, make note of anything you have in common with prospects. It will be easy to strike up a conversation about those things later and build rapport. For instance, if your prospect mentions he's a sports fan or enjoys golf, and you share the same sentiment.

Priorities: What is most important to your prospect? Did he mention a gripe with his current vendor? Or something he is looking for when considering switching? Take note of this because it will help you tailor your presentation.

Behavioral type: Assessing prospects' behavioral type can be tricky, especially when you've only spent a few moments speaking with them. You may not be certain, but it's smart to record your best guess as well as your reasoning behind your guess.

When to follow up: This is a big one. (In a later chapter we will go over some script options for how to ask this question.) In the meantime, keep assessing a follow-up timeline however you've been doing it, but make sure you record a concrete date. It's also good to make a note of the best time to call. For B to B it might not matter as long as it's during business hours, but for B to C, it's good to get a general idea of when your prospect is available. If you've already asked a lot of questions, this one should be lower on your list. You can always record when you called and use that for picking a good follow-up time later.

Did the call turn into an appointment?: This is a metric often used to gauge success or productivity. Getting in-person meetings is great, but you want to focus on motivated prospects. We will discuss prequalifying more in a later chapter, but for now, make sure you track which calls turn into in-person meetings.

Now that we've identified a bunch of things you should take notes on during your calls, how will you remember them all? Great question. A lot of companies have a form for salespeople to use, or required fields already marked in their CRM system. If that's the case for you, maybe this list can help spark ideas for any helpful additions to what you've been recording already. If your company doesn't have anything like this in place already, you can make your own form or tracking sheet. Use Word or Excel to type up your checklist. If you write notes by hand, print your checklist and take notes directly on the paper.

The point here is that it doesn't really matter how you remember to record the items on your checklist, but that you develop a system that works for you so you get it done for every single call.

A SYSTEM FOR FOLLOW UP

Now that you've recorded when to follow up, you just need to remember to do it! This is where CRM systems can make your life a whole lot easier. When you record your notes for each call, any good CRM system will allow you to choose a date to follow up. When that date comes, following up with that particular prospect will be on your task list or to-do list for the day. All you have to do is work your way through that list of calls, using the excellent notes you already took to remind you of all the details you need when calling prospects back. This is hands down, the easiest system for following up with prospects.

If you don't have a CRM system, don't despair. You have other options. (Aside from begging your manager to get a CRM system because it will help everyone at your company be more effective and sell more.) Depending on how many prospects you call and the scope of your follow-up needs, you can enter calls directly into your calendar or to-do list. If you use Outlook, Google Calendar, or a similar online system, you can enter notes on specific days and get reminders. If you're old school and don't use electronic calendars, that's fine, but you'll need to get a really good hardcopy day planner. The Covey Planner is a popular one because it features daily task lists, priority items, and extra space for notes.

Whether you decide on using a CRM system, online calendar, or hardcopy planner, make sure you give yourself reminders of who to call on what days. You should have one single place to look each day that tells you exactly what calls you need to make. If you don't develop this system, you will be lost. I promise. Even if you don't have many prospects to track right now, it's really easy to overlook a note you made last month to check in with someone. And losing the easy sale is the most painful. Aside from that, you don't want to worry about trying to remember who to call. Remember one of the first pieces of advice I gave at the beginning of this chapter? Don't even try to commit the details of your prospecting calls to memory. It won't be pleasant and it won't work anyway.

Your note-taking and follow-up systems are probably the most important systems you will develop. Without them, you won't be prepared for follow-up calls. I don't know about you, but about 70 percent of my business comes from calling prospects I've already spoken with. If I didn't have great systems for taking notes, tracking conversations, and calling people back at the right times, I would not be where I am today. Actually, I probably wouldn't even be in sales because I wouldn't be making enough to support myself and feel good about my career. It took me some time to develop my systems, but they were a lifesaver once I got the hang of them.

PLAY BOX EXERCISE: TEST YOUR NOTE-TAKING AND FOLLOW-UP SYSTEMS

Now it's time to test your systems! I recognize that readers will be at different places in the creation or evolution of their systems, but the point of this exercise is to step it up a notch. Think about your current systems. What's working well and what could be improved? Here are a few questions to help guide your thinking:

» Do I know which prospects to follow up with each day?

» Is it easy for me to find notes from the last time I spoke with a client?

» After reading my notes, do I understand how to approach the next call?

» Am I using the technology that is available to me?

» Is my current system taking longer than necessary?

_____

_____

_____

_____

_____

Considering these questions, write down a couple of things you could do to improve your systems. For example, if you have a CRM system but you aren't using it the way I described, you should make an effort to become familiar with the functionality. Start slowly, maybe just a couple of calls at a time, but force yourself to use it regularly so you get comfortable with it. As another example, if you take notes during calls but don't set reminders for following up, figure out how you want to start doing that. If you want to use a hardcopy planner, buy one today. If you want to use your Outlook Calendar, view a tutorial of adding tasks. Then, start adding follow-up calls to your to-do list on specific days. You can start slowly so you aren't overwhelmed. Whatever your situation, you should know where you can improve. Write down your goals below to hold yourself accountable. Start taking action today!

A BETTER TIME-MANAGEMENT SYSTEM

To Do Lists: In addition to your daily follow-up call list, you should have a general to-do list. Make sure you set a little time aside to work on your daily to-do list, either the night before or first thing in the morning. Also know that not everything on your to-do list is of equal importance. Some tasks will be urgent and definitely need to get done that day, whereas others could be done if you still have time left after finishing your most important tasks.

While to-do lists are very useful tools, let's not ignore the gratification that comes with them. Seriously, how good does it feel to cross things off of your list and know you don't have to worry about them anymore? I'm not proud to admit it, but there have been times in the past when I did something I realized wasn't on my list and I'd write it down just so I could cross it off. This feeling of accomplishing to-dos releases endorphins in the body and knocks down stress one tiny notch at a time. It's also gratifying to be reminded of all of the things you accomplished at the end of the day.

Administrative Support: You'll notice that some of the tasks on your to-do list have to be done by you personally, whereas others just need to get done. As you advance in your role, you may have the luxury of getting your own assistant, and that frees up a lot of your time to focus on what you do best—speaking and meeting with clients. If you aren't to that point yet but you still need help accomplishing everything on your to-do list, your colleagues may feel the same way. A great answer could be to work with a sales support professional, also known as an administrative assistant. These individuals are often the best help you can get for better managing your time.

The Power of Time-Blocking: A few years ago I heard someone say, "If it's not in your calendar it doesn't exist." That always stuck with me. Have you ever noticed that when you put something in your calendar, you actually do it? Whether it's a workout class, dinner with a friend, or a department meeting, when it's on your calendar, you show up. Why? First, because you remembered to do it. Second, because you planned on doing it at one point and now the act of doing it is automatic. Unless you're in a real jam, you don't think about rescheduling. You just get it done.

Most people consider their calendars as tools for reserving time with other people. Chances are, most of the appointments on your calendar involve interacting with another person in some way, even if it's just a reminder to go to yoga. If this is how you use your calendar, you're missing out on a major time management and productivity trick: time blocking appointments with yourself. I got into the habit of doing this while I was working at KW, and it's helped me a ton.

The idea behind time blocking is to reserve set amounts of time for the tasks you need to complete. During each time block, you focus on the task at hand and don't allow yourself to get sidetracked by anything else. This system is especially effective for the tasks you are prone to putting off because it doesn't allow you to procrastinate. It's also great for making sure the day doesn't get away from you where suddenly it's 5 o'clock and you didn't do the most important things on your to-do list for that day.

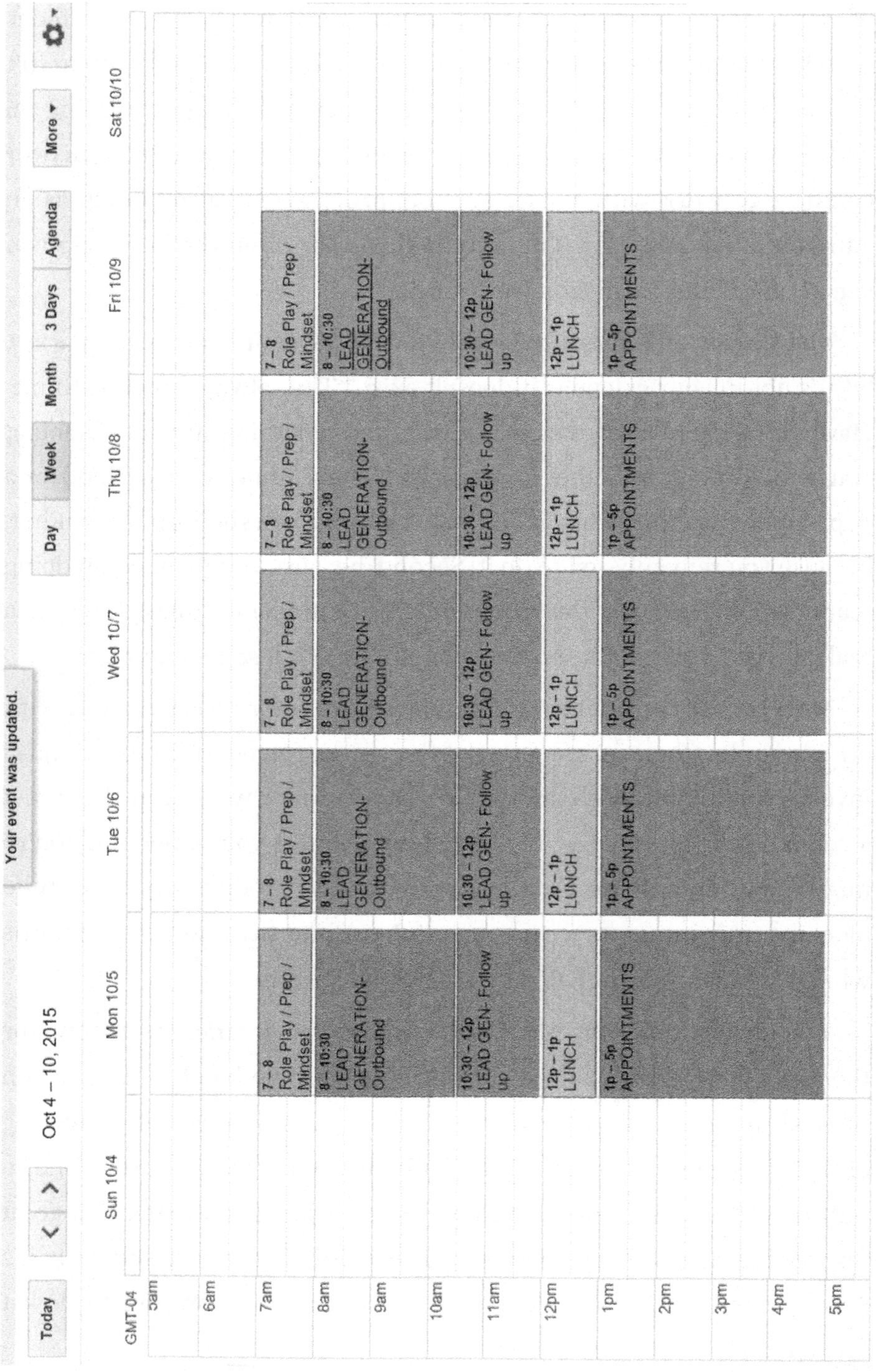
Today
Oct 4 – 10, 2015
Your event was updated.
Day
Week
Month
3 Days
Agenda
More ▾
GMT-04
Sun 10/4
Mon 10/5
Tue 10/6
Wed 10/7
Thu 10/8
Fri 10/9
Sat 10/10
5am
6am
7am
8am
9am
10am
11am
12pm
1pm
2pm
3pm
4pm
5pm
7 – 8 Role Play / Prep / Mindset
8 – 10:30 LEAD GENERATION- Outbound
10:30 – 12p LEAD GEN- Follow up
12p – 1p LUNCH
1p – 5p APPOINTMENTS

Time blocking also enables you to increase your productivity by scheduling tasks when you typically feel most productive and focused. For me, as well as most people, I'm in "work mode" in the morning. That's why I always time block 8am-11am to make my calls. I know that whatever happens later in the day, I have my most important tasks finished.

I recommend that you pay attention to your energy and body rhythms throughout the day and time block your calls for when you feel most focused, but I bet it will be in the morning. Work has a way of draining our energy, just like a battery drains if it's always in use. Set yourself up for success by doing the most important work when you feel your best.

When you time block on a shared company calendar, you can set your appointments to show as "busy" instead of showing exactly what you're doing. In other words, it will look exactly the same as meetings with other people, and your co-workers will try to avoid scheduling other meetings at those times. You can also go full tilt and let your co-workers and assistants know that nothing else happens during your time blocks, and your time blocks are the same time daily. I learned this from Gary Keller.

When you travel a lot, as many salespeople do, time blocking becomes even more important for reserving the time you need for must-do tasks. It's easy to have non-urgent meetings and emails suck up any available time, but if you already have time blocked off on your calendar, it's easier to guard against losing it.

The main thing to keep in mind is that when you time block, you should take it just as seriously as you do other commitments. Yes, the times are more flexible, but the amount of time needed to complete tasks is not. If something comes up during your 8am-11am time block to make sales and follow up calls, you better make room for it later in the day.

MASTER YOUR EMAIL

Do you have a love-hate relationship with your email? If so, you aren't alone. Email is great because it helps us communicate instantly, both professionally and socially. But there is just *so* much of it. Responding to emails can feel like a job in itself. Anything can pop into your inbox and suddenly it has your attention. Sometimes it's warranted but other times it's a relentless distraction. Luckily, there are a few systems for answering emails effectively and not letting your inbox derail your productivity.

The "At-Work" Away Message: If you've ever emailed me, you know I only reply to emails twice a day—once in the morning and once before I leave the office. You know that because I have an out-of-office automated reply for all emails I receive. Here's a sample of my away message:

> » "To serve our clients best I check emails twice daily, at 11am and then again at 4pm est. I will respond to your email during those times. If you need an immediate response via email during normal business hours please email logistics@htahomes.com or call 508-871-7141. Evenings or weekends please call 508-365-3576. Thank you again for your email and understanding."

I also let my contacts know at the beginning of our relationship about my system for replying to email. They know email is important to me and I will reply in less than 24 hours, whether it's later that afternoon or the next morning. This system allows me to pretty much ignore my inbox during the day. I don't feel compelled to respond right away because people already know I will respond soon. If you're able to set up a system like this at your job, I highly recommend it. You may need to speak with your manager to get approval, but if it helps your productivity, hopefully you can get the OK.

Empty Your Inbox: There's nothing more distracting and discouraging than a cluttered inbox, yet so many people have them because they don't have a good system for filing and responding to emails. I get through almost all of my emails every single day. Two or three might sit overnight, but never more than that. A cluttered inbox drives me crazy, so I came up with a system to easily clear it out. First, I don't procrastinate responding. If I know what I need to say, I'll say it right then. Second, if it's information I don't want to think about now, but know I want to consider later, I use a Gmail add-on tool called Boomerang. I can set a specific date, and have the email come back to my inbox on that date. I Boomerang all non-urgent emails to Saturdays, or a late afternoon once a week and I time block an hour or so to deal with them.

There are also tools that allow you to hit send on an email and delay the delivery until a specified time. If I happen to answer an email during the day, sometimes I delay the delivery so people don't get used to me responding outside of my normal schedule. This tool is also helpful if you're ever responding to emails late at night. It might look weird to customers or co-workers if your email comes through at 4am, so it's best to delay it to a more reasonable time. Not that I am personally up at 4am reading emails, but I have received emails at all hours of the night and it does not look professional.

Use Templates: If you send the same type of information regularly, don't reinvent the wheel every time. Save a good "generic" version of your message, and copy and paste it into new emails as needed. The CRM system I use has an email library so I can create templates of the emails that go out frequently. This takes some time on the front end but can save you a ton of time on the back end.

All of these systems will help you better manage your emails, reduce distractions, and probably decrease your stress as well. Because let's be honest, when your email is super organized your whole life starts to feel super organized.

CHAPTER SUMMARY

Developing systems can seem like extra work in the short-term, but they will save you hundreds and hundreds of hours in the long run. If you want to be successful, it starts with being organized. As boring as that may seem, it's the truth. Luckily, if you put in the work now, you'll start realizing the benefits right away and they will only grow exponentially over time.

KEY TAKEAWAYS:

» Write everything down.

» Schedule follow-up call reminders for specific dates.

» Protect your "free" time with time blocking.

CHAPTER 5

. . . .

PLAYING TO WIN VS. PLAYING NOT TO LOSE

"You were born to win, but to be a winner, you must plan to win, prepare to win, and expect to win."

Zig Ziglar

Sometimes the best sales appointments are the ones I don't take. It took me a while to realize that, but ever since I did, I skyrocketed my career to the next level. And I have prequalifying to thank for that. If you want to take your sales career to the next level, it's kind of like they say in the Geico Insurance commercial: "Prequalifying, it's what you do!"

In a nutshell, prequalifying is the process of predicting the likelihood a prospect will buy from you, and how quickly they will do it. The idea is to focus on the prospects that are most likely to buy soon, rather than spending a lot of time trying to win over prospects that are unlikely to buy at all or any time in the near future. Prequalifying is part of the artistry of sales. And like any art form, it takes a lot of time and practice to get good at it. Prequalifying is planning to win, preparing to win and expecting to win.

Many times when people first start out in sales, they don't do any prequalifying at all. They are so happy to speak with a prospect who sounds interested that they fully pursue the lead, however long it takes to get a yes or no. To seasoned reps, this may sound unproductive, but it isn't necessarily a bad thing for sales rookies. It takes time and practice to learn the fundamentals of sales and a lot of prospecting conversations to get a good read on what a serious buyer sounds like. New salespeople don't have this experience yet, which often makes prequalifying unrealistic for them. If you're fairly new to sales or you're new to your company, don't feel bad if you aren't great at prequalifying or if you haven't done it at all. This book will teach you what you need to know to become great at prequalifying. As I learned from experience, improving starts with changing your mindset.

I didn't start prequalifying at Keller Williams until I had worked there for eight years. Up until that point, I figured I might as well go meet with anyone who sounded interested in selling his or her home. It was working pretty well, so I just kept doing it. Then I got a business coach and my approach to prequalifying was one of the first things he wanted me to change. I listened to him and learned how to prequalify my leads before deciding to meet with prospects in person, and that's when my business really took off.

I learned a valuable lesson here that I want you to take to heart. There are two different approaches to sales: *playing to win and playing not to lose.* Most people think they are playing to win, even when that's not the case.

I sure thought I was playing to win during those first eight years selling real estate at KW. I felt like I was playing to win because I was making sales and reaching many of my goals. But I realized that my mentality was wrong. Instead of trying not to lose the potential sales from people I had already talked to, I could be going after even better opportunities I hadn't found yet. That was a revelation to me. But in order to go after those better opportunities, I needed to stop investing so much time in the ones that were unlikely to pan out. Frankly, I was sacrificing personal time and time with my family for success by working 70-80 hours a week. Instead of playing not to lose, I had to start playing to win. In 2010, I became fully committed to changing my approach. At the end of one year, I realized I had made almost the same income as the prior year but I cut my hours worked by almost 40 percent.

Whether you want to cut back your hours and make the same amount or work the same amount and make a lot more, prequalifying will help you. You already know you shouldn't set out to close every prospect. If you had an endless amount of time, you could afford to pursue people who don't seem that interested and those who will take a long time to decide. But none of us have an endless amount of time, and as the saying goes, you have to pick your battles. The challenge is knowing which prospects to pursue and which to let go. If you get better at that, and I mean just a little bit better, you'll start to see results. You start out slow, build up your skills, and your outcomes will just keep getting better. It's kind of like lifting weights. If you're totally out of shape, you can't start out bench-pressing 250 Lbs. But if you lift lighter weights every day and slowly work up your strength, you can get there.

Now, if you work in some industries, you may be thinking this section doesn't apply to you because prequalifying leads is not the standard. For example, in high price tag B to B sales, prospecting can be more about building relationships with all potential clients in your territory. Sales expert and author John Chapin says that in these situations, you focus on "lead nurturing" instead of prequalifying, but in some ways it's similar. In both cases, you have a limited amount of time and resources, and you have to decide where to spend it. Chapin said when he worked in B to B sales he would always put the most effort into lead nurturing the bigger opportunities rather than the smaller ones, since he and his company stood more to gain. So if you work at a company where lead nurturing is the way to go, know that you'll still need to prequalify your prospects to know how to allocate your efforts. You'll also need to direct your efforts to the decision-maker, and determining who that person is can be considered another form of qualifying.

Essentially there is no way around prequalifying altogether. Sure, you can choose to ignore it (as I once did), but you can expect to hit a plateau and burn out pretty quickly.

KNOW WHAT TO EXPECT

The buying process will be a little different depending on the type of person you're talking to. Don't forget about using the DISC assessment or another behavioral assessment. If you can gauge your prospects' behavioral type, you'll have a better idea what to expect and how close they are to buying.

» High D: These prospects are direct and upfront about their intentions, so it should be easy to know what you're going to get. High Ds like things to move quickly and typically won't waste your time because it wastes their time as well. If you like to push through the selling process quickly, High Ds are your best bet.

» High I: These individuals like to talk. They enjoy building relationships and will want to do that to some degree before they buy from you. If it seems like you're chatting a lot without any business moving forward, remember that strong relationships and rapport fuel the decision-making process for High Is. The selling process with these individuals may take a little longer but it won't be all business, and sometimes that's nice. If your company has entertainment perks like baseball tickets or golf outings, consider saving your invitations for High Is, especially if you can tag along. (High Ds also appreciate the invitation but may pass if it does not fit in their schedule.)

» High S: These prospects are most motivated by trust. Like High Is, the High S is also people-oriented rather than task-oriented. Know that you'll have to put your time in and show you care about the High S to win their business. If you can get an in-person meeting, they are likely to work with you. (I've closed many of these individuals in person, even if they told me on the phone they weren't ready to make a decision that day.) Many gatekeepers have High S behavior, protecting their bosses.

» High C: People with this behavioral type are unlikely to do anything without first doing their research and spending time thinking about it. That's why it's smart to send a lot of information and plan on waiting a little while to hear back. High Cs don't rush into anything, so I'm usually hesitant to meet with them in person until after I know they have completed their analysis of working with me. Sometimes you'll need to have meetings earlier in the sales cycle, but don't expect a quick and easy close.

Depending on your industry, you might sell to a specific department or role within a company, or a certain industry. In that case, understanding your target market will help you get a better read on what to expect from potential customers. For example, I interviewed a woman who sells IT products and services, and her clients work in the IT department. IT professionals are typically analytical, task-oriented people. She knows that building relationships is always important, but making small talk and socializing doesn't usually top her clients' list of priorities when it comes to making purchasing decisions. Considering the DISC behavioral profiles, she can usually expect buying behavior to align with the High D or C.

When you can gauge your prospects' behavior types, it's easier to tell how serious they are about buying and better prioritize your efforts so you can play to win.

DON'T GET USED

Being the experienced sales professional you are, I'm sure you know a wealth of information about your industry, as well as the products or services you sell. That knowledge is valuable, and people want it. You'll gladly share your expertise with potential clients to help them, but sometimes people want your knowledge for free and have no intention of buying from you. This creates a tricky situation and a huge roadblock in the prequalification process because it can be hard to know when prospects are serious about working with you. You want to be professional and helpful, but you don't want to waste your time and you can't give it all away for free.

People who have never worked in sales or aren't paid by commission don't always understand the importance of your time or how you make money. This causes them to unintentionally behave in ways that can be interpreted as rude or careless. These people don't typically set out to maliciously take advantage of you or your time. But they do want something, and it's helpful for you to keep an eye out for what that might be.

Sometimes people just want you to help shed light on their situation. They want to understand what they should do to meet a need or fix a problem. However, they might not be serious about moving forward with a purchasing decision, especially after seeing the price. This happens often with complex products and services, especially those that have a custom budget. For B to C, think home renovations. For B to B, think technology products or consulting services for that would be a big upgrade from what the company currently has. Sure, there are obviously serious buyers out there in these industries, but a lot of prospects just want an expert's opinion.

When it comes to B to B sales, especially in industries that sell some type of knowledge-based service like consulting, leadership expert and author Ana Dutra says to watch out for a key phrase: *I'd like to pick your brain*. Dutra says that's how professionals often ask others for advice without having the intention of paying for it.[9] It can sound polite and even be flattering, especially when the person asking speaks highly of your expertise. But make no mistake, they want you to help them for free. If you are hoping it leads to paid work later, you could put in the time and effort, but there's no guarantee it will pan out.

Of course you know your industry best and you may need to put in more time and resources on the front end of a sale, but it's important to be aware of relationships that turn into a time suck. Dutra says it's smart to keep track of how much time you spend helping prospects or providing additional support to current clients that falls outside of your sales agreement. "When you document your time, it will be easier to see how much value you have provided to others," says Dutra. "You will be able to speak up sooner when you notice certain people taking advantage of you." When people keep asking for more support without paying for it, you can have a polite conversation and explain how you have spent X hours helping them and you are happy to be a resource, but the support you're offering is starting to feel like a project. To ensure you set aside time to best help them, you recommend a formal agreement for the work.

Another way salespeople get used is when prospects source bids from a lot of companies just for the heck of it. This can be considered background research, except when companies have no intention of switching vendors—they are only reaching out to a variety of companies because that's what their internal procedure calls for. In B to B, this is when you get a request for proposal from a company but hear from your colleagues they send one out every year and they've been with the same vendor for 15 years. In B to C, this is the bride who has already been to 23 dress shops and has yet to find the perfect gown. When you get the feeling you are dealing with a prospect like this, you don't necessarily want to consider interacting with them a waste of time, but you probably don't want to invest much time either.

As you think about prequalifying leads, keep your eyes open for situations where prospects are stringing you along with little intentions on buying. Of course you want to keep it polite and professional, but you must guard your time. After all, it is a non-renewable resource. Time can't be cheated, it is the great equalizer." All salespeople start out with 24 hours in a day, but some manage their time better than others.

SCREENING PROSPECTS

Some companies train salespeople to go heavy on prequalification. It really comes down to the expected ROI of the sales process. If most prospects fall out instead of closing and the cost of supporting the sales cycle is high, it's smart to do some serious prequalifying before you invest in pursuing leads. For example, I know a home improvement company that is basically a prequalifying machine. They have reps go door to door to ask homeowners if they are interested in a free quote for home improvement services. Those who are get a follow-up call from the "scheduling department." The scheduling reps are tasked with asking homeowners a *long* list of questions to assess two things: 1) if they are motivated to purchase home improvement services and 2) if they can afford it. If/when the prospect answers all of the questions, the scheduling rep can choose whether to send a consultant to the home in person to provide a quote. It's important for scheduling reps to get answers to all of the questions and properly assess the likelihood to close the sale because it's costly for the company to send consultants out in person.

Being so comprehensive with the prequalification process weeds out a lot of prospects. Most of them, actually. Out of the 200+ calls the scheduling reps make each day, they might set 10 in-person meetings. Prospects hang up on them all the time because they think the financial questions are too personal or the process of getting a free quote is too much work. But the company's philosophy is playing to win, which means ensuring an extremely high likelihood of closing a sale *that day* when a consultant meets with homeowners in person. The company knows that B to C selling means prospects are more likely to behave in a wishy-washy way than with B to B sales. Individual people can buy whatever they want or choose not to buy anything. They don't have to run their decisions by a team for approval and they don't have the responsibility of behaving professionally. And they often make purchasing decisions based on emotion rather than a pre-determined timeline or need. With all of that in mind, it can be incredibly hard to know who is a serious buyer, especially when you're selling something that can cost up to $50,000. That's why this company screens their prospects before pursuing them.

This level of prequalifying is unusual in many sales cycles, but it can be effective depending on what you sell. Either way, it's helpful to understand this is the reality for a lot of salespeople. You have to be comfortable playing to win.

THINKING LONG TERM

When salespeople think about prequalifying leads, it's usually with the mentality that they would want to work with all prospects, if given the chance. Most salespeople think about the amount of time and the difficulty level of closing someone, and that's how they decide which clients to pursue. But what happens after the close?

When you win new customers or clients, they often become a part of your daily reality. You get to know them and your co-workers often do too. This is especially true in industries that sell long-term support of some kind and those where employees spend a lot of time working with clients directly, like consulting. In those types of companies, you may not want to close anyone who is willing to pay you. Just like they are vetting you, you should be vetting them. This is one of the things in life that you usually have to do wrong before you appreciate the importance of doing it right.

Getting the wrong type of clients can be detrimental to a business for many reasons. The most immediate impact can be how much time and effort goes into a project. Some clients require a lot more support than others. Depending on your agreement, clients may feel they are entitled to extra support, whether that's something your company intended or not. If you don't have the bandwidth to support this unexpected project scope, it can suck the energy out of you and your team and even compromise the service you provide to other clients. Your efforts in prospecting for new business can also take a hit, since you won't have as much time to make calls. In some cases, working with a high-maintenance client can be worth the extra time and effort. (e.g., a well known, impressive name to add to your client roster or portfolio, or the project experience you need to expand into a new industry or market.) But if working with a needy client doesn't serve any additional benefits than the average client, you would have been better off focusing on closing a different prospect.

In addition to fostering positive working relationships that align with your business goals, you have to think about customer satisfaction. With the rise of online reviews, a businesses' reputation is now more important than ever. A scathing review from an unhappy customer can cause a lot of damage. While many bad reviews are a reflection of bad service, it's true that some people are harder to please than others. If a prospect is moody, fickle, or hotheaded from the beginning, what are the chances that demeanor is going to completely change later? Probably not very good. Although that person could turn into a perfectly good client, bad attitudes always raise a red flag for me as a salesperson.

One time a guy who goes to my gym approached me about selling his home. I had only talked to him occasionally in passing, but since we sort-of had a personal relationship, I decided to give him the benefit of the doubt and take the sale a little more casually than I normally would. I agreed to go out to his house that afternoon without prequalifying to take a look at the property. His house was nice, but I started getting a bad vibe from him because he was complaining about all kinds of things, especially things his last agent did or did not do. This started at the gym but continued as soon as I walked in his house. I also realized I made the mistake of not confirming that his wife would be there during the visit. Realtors typically need both decision-makers there to get hired, so after I spent about 60 minutes listening to him rant, I set another appointment to come back to the house when his wife would be there too. (At this point, the story is also an example of playing not to lose. I had invested a few hours into this prospect and now I was going to take the listing even though I got a bad vibe.)

Anyway, he pressed me for an evaluation of the home before our second meeting, saying he and his wife were very curious to know how much I thought it would sell. In my industry, this is the key way salespeople get used. That's why I only provide evaluations for people who have already agreed to work with me. But in this case I gave it to him before we signed a contract because he had agreed to schedule a second meeting.

The next morning, the guy texted me and said they were all set but appreciated my help. I called him right away, but I could tell he probably hit the side button on his phone because it rang once and went to voice-mail. I left a voicemail and called again later in the day from a different phone number and he answered right away. As soon as he found out it was me he hung up. WOW! Long story short, we didn't end up working together. A week later I found out they had put a sign out and decided to try and sell the house themselves, of course at the price I gave them.

Although I didn't get any business, I was happy with the outcome. After getting to know the guy a little, I actually felt like I dodged a bullet. Working with him would have been a nightmare because he wasn't respectful of my time and it was clear he was extremely hard to please. This one incident was my takeaway that I will always prequalify no matter what. I can thank him for that. And yes, it's kind of strange seeing him at the gym now...

If given the choice, I would rather work with a prospect who is agreeable and reasonable from the beginning, rather than one who seems ready to bite my head off. Not only will the experience be more pleasant, it's likely to yield better customer service outcomes, which translate to better outcomes for me.

Even if I did a stellar job and over-delivered for this guy, it's likely he may have only felt lukewarm about me. That's a problem. Yes, I may have been able to avoid a negative review from him, but my goal isn't to have customers who just feel so-so about me. Every time a sale ends like that, it's a lost opportunity. Why? Because I missed out on making a client so happy that he wants to go around telling everyone about me, practically shouting from the rooftops about what a great experience he had. That's how I get new warm leads. Do you think that guy would have generated new leads for me? I don't. Word of mouth marketing is one of the most effective ways to bring in new business, and every time I work with a cranky, finicky customer who is never pleased by anything, I miss out on that.

Now, you and/or your company may not currently be in a position to turn down leads from people you don't want to work with. But if it comes down to only having time to pursue a certain number of leads, you should think about what prospects will be like when they become clients. If you're an entrepreneur and you have a small business, or you're starting your own sales business within a larger company, it's especially important to get customers who love working with you. If they can give you referrals to other prospects or testimonials about how great you are to work with, it can make a huge difference in your success. That's why getting evangelical customers is always a goal when you play to win.

Your future self will thank you.

TALKING MONEY

A major part of prequalifying is determining whether your prices are in line with prospects' expectations. After all, if people can't afford to buy what you're selling, it doesn't matter how much they like you or want to buy from you. Depending on what you sell and how your company does things, you may discuss pricing at the beginning of the sales cycle or toward the end. There are a ton of different strategies for this, but one thing you may not have considered is how the phone can help.

Ashley works for a consulting firm that sells employee surveys. She says she likes to discuss pricing on the phone instead of over email because it's easier to tell if prospects think the price is manageable or too high. "With written communication, people have time to hide their true reaction," she says. "An authentic reaction on the spot is much more telling." Ashley likes to throw out a number or price range on the phone because if people react positively, she knows she doesn't have to worry about pricing. Gaining this knowledge is an important part of the prequalification process because pricing varies greatly in her industry. Prospects' budgets may not be in the ballpark for the solutions her company sells, and it's important to figure that out sooner rather than later, especially since the sales cycle can be time consuming for sales reps. There are often lengthy requests for proposals, conference calls, and in-person meetings before a company makes a hiring decision. It's best for everyone to have an honest discussion about pricing, and Ashley finds that the phone is the best tool for facilitating this.[10]

It's true that discussing pricing is generally considered one of the most uncomfortable aspects of sales, but you can't skirt around it if you're playing to win. There are a lot of ways you can frame pricing, and your goal should be to establish an idea of how much customers can expect to pay, and are willing to pay. If your prices range depending on a lot of factors, make sure you explain that the number or range you quote is just a starting point. Maybe it's an example of what another customer pays for a slightly smaller or larger project. Or maybe it's the basic price, but you can offer a more competitive deal for a longer contract. When it comes to pricing, people like options, and it's easy to communicate this quickly and effectively over the phone.

In real estate every once in a while I would get someone who was insistent on getting a value from me before meeting, so I would always say, "The market shows a range of x to x, but I would need to see the house in order to determine a closer value."

If you sell something that's on the expensive side, using the phone to discuss pricing is even better because you can redirect the conversation back to the superior value you provide. Remember how we talked about tone being ambiguous over email? This is true for pricing as well. If you send over a contract that has a $10,000 quote, the prospect may scroll to the end of the document, see the total and go into sticker shock. (Yes, numbers can feel like they are screaming at you sometimes!) Instead of reading the whole document to understand all of the value you provide, he might delete your quote and move onto the next email. If you were to talk to the same prospect on the phone, you could ease him into the pricing by saying you charge a bit more than other companies, but it's because he will receive so much more support. You could give the exact same $10,000 quote without it feeling like a hit to the gut. It reminds me of the saying, "it isn't what you say, it's how you say it." The price might not be what turns people off; it's how the price is presented. With this in mind, you can see how a little finesse on the phone can go a long way.

Bottom line, it's important to know if pricing or other factors may be a deal-breaker for closing a sale. This gives you a choice: you can still meet with the person and at least you know what you're going into or you could decide to focus on better leads. I will always remember watching a presentation given by one of the top salespeople in the U.S. and hearing him say, "The purpose of prequalification is to find a better appointment." That's how you play to win. And that's why some of my best appointments are the ones I don't take.

ASKING PROSPECTS IF THEY ARE READY TO BUY

How do you know if a prospect is motivated to buy? Well, you could just go ahead and ask. If the thought of that makes you cringe, you definitely are not alone. Luckily, you can get to the heart of this question without being rude or obnoxious. Of course the script here will depend on what you're selling, but the basic framework can be applied to all industries.

» Tone: Make an extra effort to sound calm and pleasant when you ask. Don't sound impatient like the prospect is wasting your time.

» Come from a point of contribution: If people wonder why you're asking, explain that it's helpful to know their interests and goals so you can better serve them. Coming from contribution is making the whole process about them.

Following those rules, here's an example of what I would usually say in real estate: "If everything we talk about tomorrow makes sense and you feel comfortable and confident in my abilities do you plan to hire me tomorrow when I come out?"

The first time I asked that question, I could hardly get it to come out of my mouth. I felt weird asking and I wasn't sure how the prospect would take it. He paused for a moment and said, "Ummm... yeah I guess." I thought "Woohoo!" and had to compose myself to keep from saying it out loud and laughing from relief. I felt like a huge weight lifted off of my shoulders. It was so easy! I didn't know that all I had to do was ask. Obviously, prospects don't always say yes, but then I can ask other questions about what would ultimately make them feel comfortable working with me. Then, at least I know what objections I have to deal with when meeting them.

SUMMARY

Playing to win isn't just a way of going about your job; it's a state of mind. When you adopt it, you'll become more efficient and successful. Better still, you won't worry when opportunities don't work out as you hoped, because you'll just move right on to the next one. Remember, your time is money, and prequalifying will help you protect it. And make more of it!

KEY TAKEAWAYS:

» Go after the best opportunities: Prequalify to prioritize

» Don't get used: Track the time you spend helping prospects and clients for free

» Talk pricing: Get on the same page with prospects to ensure you aren't wasting each other's time

CHAPTER 6

· · · · · · · · · ·

THE ROAD TO MASTERY

"I do not fear the man with 10,000 kicks. I fear the man who has practiced one kick 10,000 times."

Bruce Lee

"The more I practice, the luckier I get."

Arnold Palmer

When you think about the people who have become "the greats" in their lines of work (e.g., Michael Phelps, Leonardo da Vinci, Mozart, and Kobe Bryant), do you ever wonder what made them so successful? Yes, they all have natural talent, but many people are born with talent and never find success, let alone international recognition for their talents. In the fields of swimming, painting, composing music, and playing basketball, there have been many success stories and many impressive outcomes from a multitude of people over the years. But individuals such as these seem to rise easily above the crowd of their successful peers. Why? Well, they all have something else in common besides talent: they put in more hours honing their skills than anyone else. All of these greats are actually known for the amount of practice and work they made an ongoing part of their careers.

"Give me six hours to chop down a tree and I will spend the first four sharpening the axe."

Abraham Lincoln

Let's take Michael Phelps for example. When he was training for the Olympics and other races, he practiced three hours per day. Most elite and professional athletes take one day off each week, but Phelps practiced every single day. He realized that by practicing on Sundays, he would get about 50 extra days of practice per year than his competitors. Under the advice of his coach, he also practiced extensively with his goggles full of water. He wanted to be prepared in case his goggles came loose during a race. If you remember the 200-butterfly at the 2008 Beijing Olympics, Phelps' goggles did fill up with water, something that could easily cost a swimmer the race. But Phelps had practiced that way so much already it was like second nature to him and he won the race without being able to see anything for about the last 100 meters.[11] He prepared at a level so far beyond his competitors that in 2008 at the Beijing Olympics he took home eight gold medals, setting a record for the most golds won by an Olympian in a single year. In 2012, he became the most winning Olympian of all time in any sport, with 22 medals, 18 of them gold.[12]

Is Michael Phelps the best swimmer who ever walked the earth? Maybe. But if you think of all of the people over the years who have had the *potential* to be a world-class swimmer, Phelps certainly isn't alone. However, throughout history, most people haven't chosen to invest in the resources or time that Phelps had to practice. Three hundred years ago, good old Marco from Naples could have been known as the fastest swimmer in the land, but he still had to hold down a paying job to feed his family. Could Marco have been the fastest swimmer ever if he had the ability to practice three hours a day seven days a week for years in a real pool? Quite possibly. Phelps may seem like he has the talents of a superhero, but realistically, he's chosen to practice his skills more than anyone else. Practice transformed him from being a person who had potential into a legend.

Don't get me wrong—I'm not discounting Phelps' talents or anyone else's. I'm just making the point that practice is the real difference-maker in success. When you put in the time, you will get results. When you look at all of the most successful people, like Bryant, Mozart, or da Vinci, no one can say they got there by luck. They all put in thousands upon thousands of hours of work. And when they were close to the top or even at the very top, becoming pillars of success in their fields, they kept working. The sheer number of hours spent developing a very specific set of skills elevated them to a level of mastery. You can do the same thing with sales.

Richard Marcinko, author of *The Rogue Warrior* and leader of a Navy Seals team says, "The more you sweat in training the less you bleed in combat." I know most salespeople are not dealing with life and death situations, but I always share this quote when I teach because I feel it is so powerful. The more we practice our scripts and dialogues the less likely we are going to get caught off guard by a client.

Robert Greene delves into the power of practice in his book *Mastery*. He says that when you practice a certain skill for hours upon hours, executing that particular action becomes as hardwired as a part of your nervous system. Your intuition takes over and your actions become automatic. You are a personification of a well-oiled machine. Getting this kind of result only comes from dedicating thousands of hours.

As salespeople, we can learn a lot from the masters. First and foremost, their stories put practice into perspective. If you're wondering why you aren't selling more or closing prospects quicker, chances are, you haven't spent nearly as much time practicing these skills as masters have. It really comes down to time on task. If you put the time in, you will get better.

With this in mind, you have two options:

» You can feel discouraged by the amount of work in front of you.

» You can feel encouraged because you know you'll achieve the results you're after if you put in the time and work.

You have a choice to make. Will you embrace the road to mastery or will you resist it? Thinking back to what we've covered already on mindset, you know how important it is to approach your work with a positive attitude. Your attitude is your fuel that keeps you motivated during all of those hours of practice. In this way, don't think that sales is any different from other professions. If you want to become truly great at something, anything, you have to conquer all negative emotions that could get in your way, such as boredom or frustration, and put in the time.

PRACTICE: YOU'RE PROBABLY DOING IT WRONG

Now that you understand what a little sweat and hard work can do for your career, you just need to know *how* to practice. From my experience, many organizations start off with the wrong approach in training. All too often, companies see failures from sales rookies as a right of passage rather than something that can be prevented or significantly decreased. Sure, you win some and you lose some, but you're going to lose more if this is your strategy for practicing. It's true that salespeople will become more effective as time passes, but they don't have to start at zero. This is the mistake companies make when they train new employees through observation instead of practice.

For example, there is a high chance brand new salespeople will blow a big sale because they don't know what they're doing. Companies know this and often avoid giving new salespeople big opportunities, or they pair them up with experienced salespeople. The experienced rep will either do all the work while the new person watches, or he will be there to take over when the new rep starts to falter. This is often considered good practice for sending new reps out on sales calls by themselves. However, using observation alone, it takes a long time to get salespeople to where they need to be to go off on their own with confidence and the skills necessary to get good results. Their first attempts use potential customers as guinea pigs.

I've seen whole sales organizations crumble to the ground from relying on this method of training. If everyone has to buddy up to go out on calls, the seasoned salespeople can't keep up with their normal workload because they're always helping newer reps. And instead of advancing their skills, rookie salespeople lean on tenured co-workers like a crutch, never learning to stand on their own two feet. When they do go out alone, they still feel like they aren't ready, and they don't usually do that well. (Shadowing can be valuable for salespeople, but it isn't a replacement for other types of practice or training.)

When you break it down this way, it's easy to see why this methodology is flawed, but it's astounding how often it happens. Although newer salespeople are putting in time working with prospects and observing sales meetings, this on-the-job training doesn't give them the opportunity to take the lead going through the sales motions. Watching someone else do something does not count as practice. To truly learn something and get better at it, you have to do it yourself. Repeatedly.

Yes, it will be ugly at first. That's why you can't practice on prospects. There's a decent chance you will blow sale after sale, which is painful for you and your manager. To get better at sales without wasting perfectly good leads, you have to do what's called *deliberate practice*. Based on education research dating back thousands of years, combined with modern scientific studies, researchers have discovered the elements that support optimal learning and lead to improvement at various tasks. Swedish psychologist and expertise expert K. Anders Ericsson identified four essential components of deliberate practice:

1. You must be motivated and exert effort to improve your performance during the practice session.

2. The type of practice should take into account your pre-existing knowledge so that you understand what to do after a brief period of instruction.

3. You need immediate feedback on your performance from someone who is knowledgeable in the task or skill you're practicing.

4. You should repeatedly perform the same or similar practice exercises.[13]

Based on numerous studies, these are the components needed for practice to really make a difference. This holds true whether you're a basketball player, violinist, or a salesperson.

Now, there's a good chance you can already see how you could improve your practice, but I'm going to point out the biggest opportunities I've seen from my experience.

First, nowhere in the list of essential components does it say that you should be enjoying yourself. In fact, it's easy to see how the opposite may be the case, since practice is clearly hard work. When you're focused and trying your best to improve, the experience is much different than casual practice. Kobe Bryant doesn't joke around with teammates and goof off during practice; he's too busy trying to make 800 jump shots.[14] When you practice at this level, you can be sure gratification will come, but it might not be during your practice sessions.

Second, you're probably underestimating what's meant by "repetition." Sure, it's a vague term that means different things depending on the context. If your car got a flat tire, it might only need to happen two or three times before you start telling people you are "repeatedly" getting flats. If a salesperson called you about joining a new gym, it might only take a handful of calls before you feel like she's "repeatedly" calling you. (More on making repeated follow-up calls a little later!) Sometimes events can seem like they happen a lot if you don't really expect them to happen at all. Instead of seeing the events for what they are—a couple of occurrences—it's easy to get the feeling that they happen regularly. If your expectations for practicing are low, you probably think you're doing it often enough already. Granted I don't know how much time you spend practicing, but I'd be willing to guess you don't do it often enough to pass component number four.

After decades in sales, I still practice every single weekday. I work with my colleagues to role-play different scenarios with prospects on the phone, and I spend at least 15 minutes doing it each day. We practice common objections for some of the calls we have scheduled each day so that we're more prepared to make those calls later. Although I role-play with salespeople I manage, I'm not going through these exercises just to improve their skills. I'm doing it to improve my skills too.

The road to mastery doesn't just end when you "arrive." Building experience isn't enough to sustain your skill level, no matter how good you are. You need to keep flexing your muscles during deliberate practice.

"The future belongs to those who learn more skills and combine them in creative ways."

Robert Greene, Mastery

BOOT CAMP

I recently started a sales training boot camp to help salespeople improve their skills on the phone. Not surprisingly, the foundation of my program is based on practice. The boot camp has been extremely helpful for participants because it's so different from what they normally experience on the job. Instead of learning through trial and error and losing sales, they prepare and practice so they're ready for anything and they can close effectively.

In this section, I'll share some of the key exercises and tips from my boot camp. These are tried and true methods for elevating your sales performance.

SCRIPTS

Chances are, you either love or hate scripts. For those who hate them, I admit, the concept can seem a little weird at times. Many people say they don't want to sound scripted or canned. Instead of letting a conversation unfold naturally, a script supplies you with specific things to ask or say in various situations, which keep you on track and focused. Maybe those remarks aren't what you would naturally say. Instead of responding like you would in a normal conversation, it's an entirely different interaction that can initially feel forced. If this is your perspective, I see where you're coming from. There are certainly challenges with using scripts, but you'll soon see the benefits far outweigh the challenges. I know this for a fact: learning a script will make you sound like you know what you're talking about. Scripts keep you on track and help you sound clear, professional and intelligent about what you're selling.

If you're trying to avoid scripts altogether, you should know that it's impossible anyway. We all have our scripts: doctors, lawyers, police officers, and everyone in between. We all get into the habit of saying the same types of things in certain situations. The only difference is that sometimes scripts are well thought out and analyzed, and other times people speak off the cuff without considering how their words are interpreted. When people wing it, they often come across as insincere, inauthentic, unprofessional, and in many cases, like a buffoon. Since salespeople are in the business of winning people over, it's in your best interest to communicate effectively. The best tool for this is scripts. The key to mastering scripts is simple: Memorize, Internalize, Customize.

Memorize: You won't have time to shuffle through papers to find the correct response and read it to prospects. You really must memorize what you're supposed to say. Wait, I know what you're thinking. If you're going to customize the scripts, why don't you do that before you memorize them? Wouldn't that be more efficient? No, because it might not work as well. You might manipulate the script and change or delete the part that made it most effective. A lot of salespeople customize scripts before they even try them, and it's a mistake. They compromise what they want to say and what the company wants them to say and they end up with something weird. Trust me, I am the guy who did it my way for years, and it was weird. Memorize first.

When joining my boot camp, one of the first things new reps say when introduced to scripts is, "But that doesn't sound like me." I say, "Exactly. That's the point. It sounds like what works." We get some laughs from the group, but I smile and explain how I'm not trying to cut down anyone's style, I'm just sharing a proven formula for making sales. Until salespeople understand what works and why, they should follow the formula before they focus on their own style. This works for both the new salesperson and the seasoned salesperson who sells a new product or service.

Internalize: When you internalize something, it goes a step beyond memorization. It doesn't sound like you're reading a script anymore because you know the information so well. This is often the difference between bad and good acting. Bad actors memorize their lines and good actors internalize the words, becoming the characters. Think back to when you saw the movie *Braveheart*. Was there any point in the movie when you said to yourself, "Mel Gibson sounds like he is reading a script"? I can confidently say no. But he probably did when he first got the script. When you think of internalizing, think of what Oscar-winning actor Sir Anthony Hopkins said: "What I do is just go over and over and over my lines and learn the script so well that I can just be easy and relaxed. That's the way I always work."[15]

Customize: When you know the script well enough that it sounds like your own original thoughts, you can successfully customize it. You can swap out words here and there or try emphasizing a different aspect of the message. If you always get tongue-tied in the same place, try rewording it. Or if you can't bear to say the same cheesy thing one more time, try something else and see if the results are just as good or even better. My friend worked at a call center for frozen foods and one of the first lines of the company's script was, "Your husband enjoys good meat, doesn't he, Mrs. Johnson?" As instructed, my friend started out using the script, but untimely, she didn't want to say that line anymore so she tested other questions instead. And who can blame her? She changed that part of the script, but it wasn't until afterward that she realized how clever the original was. The line about good meat actually worked largely because it was such a weird, random question to ask people that it made prospects pause and think about how to respond.

My friend didn't personally like the quirkiness of the line, but it wasn't necessarily a negative thing. This helps show that opportunity to customize is something you earn through practice. So if you truly hate saying something, you can try changing it once you understand what purpose it serves.

If you follow these steps, the final product will be something that not only works, but also makes you feel at ease when you're making calls. This is similar to the method that is taught at Keller Williams, and in my opinion, a main reason why the company is routinely named by *Training Magazine* as one of the top training organizations in any industry year after year.

When salespeople don't like scripts, it's usually because they haven't made it through one of the three steps or they did the steps in the wrong order. The biggest challenge, as you might already realize, is that there is a learning curve with scripts. When you first try to use them, it feels unnatural. Salespeople get turned off by this feeling and they think it's a bad sign. Instead of recognizing the learning curve, they think practice won't make it any better. Fear makes people come to ridiculous conclusions sometimes. Think about playing a new sport for the first time. Holding a baseball bat and wearing a glove probably felt (and looked) awkward. But most people don't walk off the field on day one, saying they are sure the awkwardness will never subside. (For those who do try to quit on their first day, their parents often shove them back out there assuring them they just need to practice.) If you want to get good at scripts and better at sales in general, you need to put time into your scripts.

I like to think of a script as the highway. Your goal is to stay on the road, but sometimes prospects will make you veer off in another direction. They may say something that you are not prepared for and pull you off to the right side or go on a tangent and pull you off to the left side. It's

OK to go off road with them a bit to respond to concerns, but you need to stay in control. Your goal is always to get back on the highway because that is how you will reach your destination. The bottom line is that when you know your scripts, you are in control of the call.

BUT WHAT IF YOUR COMPANY DIDN'T GIVE YOU SCRIPTS?

Great question. Many companies don't. Instead of scripts, you might have been trained on general information about the company and top selling points of the products or services. That stuff is helpful, but it's really best to have some scripts as well. If you find yourself in this scenario, you should create your own scripts to memorize. I recommend creating about a dozen short scripts to start a conversation and respond to the most common objections. Talk to your top-selling co-workers and ask them what they say. How do they respond to various objections? What really works well for them? Hopefully the culture at your organization supports teamwork and co-workers aren't so competitive that they don't want to help each other. The truth is that when the whole sales team does well, the company does well, and that is better for everyone.

PLAY BOX EXERCISE: WHY SHOULD I HIRE YOU?

You will get some form of this question no matter what you sell, and you need to have a strong and concise answer ready. This isn't the time to go on a five-minute tangent about the wealth of benefits you offer clients. It's a direct question that deserves a direct answer. That's why you need to prepare some powerful answers and practice them. In the space below, write down bullet points for the top three reasons someone should hire you. Take your time to really think through this.

_____

_____

_____

_____

_____

Next, take the reasons you wrote down and work them into a one or two-sentence response. I always advise salespeople to keep it to six seconds. Yes, it's short, but you just need to pique the prospect's interest and you can elaborate as needed from there. For instance, in real estate when someone asks me this question I simply say, "I negotiate like a bulldog for my clients, which gets them more!" Do you see how it's concise, clear, and explains the benefits to clients? Remember, you always want to frame your response around what's in it for clients. Write down your response here.

Practice these scripts regularly in role-play until you master them. You want to be prepared to use them when it counts!

PLAY CALL ONE-LINERS

It's helpful to have short, one-line scripts prepared for when people tell you they aren't interested. After prospects say this, you only have a couple of seconds before they hang up. If you have some good responses ready to go, you can reply back quickly and get them to keep talking. Here are a few you should memorize, internalize, and customize:

Prospect: "I'm not interested."

» "Before you hang up..."

   » This is what I usually start with when I get this reply. Many times this will catch the prospect's attention and get you a few extra seconds. Next, you can ask an open-ended question.

» "Is that because you don't know what I do or did I catch you at a bad time?"

» I actually asked that question and had a guy say, "Listen I am working on the Ebola virus right now and can't talk. Call me back in a few weeks." Of course stopping Ebola is more important than answering a sales call! I called him back a few weeks later just like he asked, and I got his business.

» "When would be a better time to check back?"

>> You can assume they are busy rather than uninterested. Many times people will tell you to call back at a certain time. When people say that, I always ask for their email address. About 50 percent will give it to me, and then I put them in an email campaign for follow up.

Prospect: "I'm happy with what I have," or "We are happy with our current situation."

» "Excellent, Sir. I was happy with my VCR until the DVD player came out." or "I was happy with a Walkman until I discovered the iPod." (Make sure you smile here so the prospect hears that your tone is jovial, not condescending.) "If you knew there was a greater benefit with our services would you at least like to know about it?"

>> You want prospects to think differently about avoiding change and prompt them with a question that will get a yes.

Prospect: "We are not making any changes."

» "I understand. It can be a daunting task to make a lot of changes. If you were 100 percent certain a change was in your best interest, would you make it?"

>> Again, frame change in a positive light and ask a question where saying no would feel silly.

Prospect: "I'm busy right now," or "Now isn't a good time."

» "I apologize, Sir." (The apology should disarm them.) "What time works better tomorrow?" or "Sorry to interrupt. When should I follow up again? Great. What's your email?"

> » This is a difficult objection because it's hard to tell whether the prospect is actually busy or they just don't like to tell people no. Always assume they want to talk another time and ask for their email if you don't already have it.

Prospect: "Take me off your list."

» "I can definitely do that Ma'am. I'm just curious, are you familiar with the benefits we offer?"

> » You want to be respectful, but asking this question can help start a conversation. But when prospects still insist on being taken off your list, it's important (ethically and legally) to respect their wishes.

These one-liners don't work all of the time, but they do work sometimes. Don't be that salesperson who tries them a couple of times and gets discouraged. The road to mastery isn't a quick journey. You need to keep practicing and work on your delivery. As you improve you will see how overcoming quick objections can be the difference-maker in getting certain sales. Above all, remember that when people hang up, they would have done that anyway if you hadn't had pushed a little. You have nothing to lose in trying to keep the conversation going.

PLAY BOX EXERCISE: OBJECTION HANDLERS FOR SCRIPTS

Talk with the top-producing sales reps and figure out the most common objections they deal with on a regular basis. (Not the generic objections in the prior section. You want the objections from prospects who know about what you sell.) In just about any industry you will find out there are only five or six common objections and a few other less-common ones. Write down the objections, and brainstorm to come up with three different handlers for each objection. In the three responses, you want to take different approaches to handling objections because certain types of responses work better for certain types of people.

Here is an example for a new salesperson.

Prospect: "You're brand new to your role. I'm worried you don't have enough experience."

Sales rep:

1. "I am newer in the business, but my company offers amazing training and support. We all work together as a team so you can feel comfortable you will receive efficient service with a whole network of experienced professionals."

2. "I understand your concern, but I see it as an advantage. I have fewer clients so I can offer you more time and service than many of the other reps."

3. "I certainly appreciate your concern, but can assure it won't be an issue. I will bring excitement and high energy to your project, which is something many of the other reps no longer possess."

You can see how High D prospects will probably respond best to the first script because they are worried about wasting time. High Is might like the second or third script the best because they want someone who is excited about their project and ready to build a good relationship. The challenge is knowing the scripts well enough that they are internalized and you can quickly and easily pick which one would work the best in each situation.

This is hard work. Think of it as developing a foundational skillset for selling on the phone, rather than a simple exercise you can master right away.

_____

_____

_____

_____

_____

_____

Re-write the objections in your journal or notebook then write three objection handlers for each objection.

RULES FOR ROLE-PLAY

Role-playing is the best vehicle for practicing your scripts and general skills on the phone. As I mentioned, I still do it every day. Even if my co-workers are in the office next to mine, we still call each other on the phone to role-play instead of doing it in person. That way, the practice closely resembles what real sales calls are like.

We do a lot of role-playing in my sales training boot camp. Participants spend 30 minutes role-playing on the phone every single day before making real calls to prospects. I pair up different people each day so that participants get to experience speaking with a diverse group of people. This allows them to get familiar with various personalities and behavioral types, and pick up on nuances in conversations.

If role-playing isn't the norm at your organization, talk to your manager about making it a regular exercise. Any good manager will be pleased to see a salesperson take that kind of initiative to improve. Alternately, if your co-workers are slammed or your sales team is more like a one-man band where you're the star, you can ask a personal friend to role-play with you instead. I also encourage my participants to role-play with salespeople in different industries. That way it gives you a different perspective. In one of my boot camps, I had a team of multi-level marketing reps role-playing with both real estate and mortgage professionals. We tell them to just be yourself and at the end, let me know how you felt. It's that simple.

As you role-play and practice your scripts, make sure you're also working on the skills we covered in Chapter 2 that help you connect with people over the phone. (Mirror and match, work on your intonation, vary your speaking pace, use the "you know..." trick phrase, use your active-listening Mmm Hmmm, and don't forget to tell stories that show your expertise in action.)

When each call ends, make sure you either give or get feedback on what went well and what could be improved. As you know, this is a key aspect of deliberate practice. A great way to give constructive feedback is a technique I got from Toastmasters International called the sandwich approach. Tell them something they did well, something they could do better, and wrap it up with something else they did well. The criticism is sandwiched between compliments, which makes it easier to digest.

Role-playing is great because it serves as a test drive for various responses you might get from prospects. Sometimes you won't have a script that specifically corresponds to a response, and you'll need to improvise. This usually goes smoother if you've taken a crack at that response before during role-play. As an example, one time I called a lady and she said, "I don't have time to take your call right now." She caught me off guard and my natural response was, "You just did." She promptly hung up. I sat there thinking that I had obviously responded really poorly and wondered how those words just came out of my mouth. In role-play, her exact phrasing must not have come up and I was thrown off by the wording. It only took one time of saying that to learn to never do it again. But it would have been nice to learn it during practice instead of on a real sales call! The next time I hear, "I don't have time to take your call right now," I will respond with a better response of, "Oh, I'm sorry. What is a better time to call you back?"

Another way I am deliberate with role-play is to be difficult. My goal is to make selling more challenging for salespeople in the role-play sessions than it would be in real life, but we work up to that point. We start off easier and as they learn I get more and more difficult. That's how they grow! Similar to Michael Phelps' coach, I'm sure that the first few practices were not with his goggles full of water.

SUMMARY

No one starts out knowing exactly what to do without ever having done it before. That's why practicing is essential for your success. The more time and effort you put into practicing, the more you'll increase your skills and the more you'll sell.

The goal is to get to a point where your work is intuitive. I've been selling homes for so long that I can almost always predict which prospects will close, for me and for my team. Colleagues will come to me and tell me about a situation with a prospect and I already have a good sense of whether it'll go through or not, and why. I can tell people when I foresee a problem that will become a roadblock and when everything will work out. Less experienced salespeople have even gone so far as to call me *the Yoda of Sales* or *Mr. Wolf*, the infamous problem-solver from the movie *Pulp Fiction*. Although it's flattering, my success really boils down to putting in the time and effort to practice and truly master something. When you spend enough time developing a skillset, it becomes second nature. Compared with how I felt 20 years ago, selling seems much easier because I'm better at it. Don't get me wrong—there are still day-to-day challenges. However, I am in a much more confident and secure place in my life because I have developed this expertise.

And I'm not any different from you. If you put in the time and effort, it *will* pay off. I promise.

KEY TAKEAWAYS

» Practice Deliberately: Follow the four components

» Use Scripts: Memorize, Internalize, Customize (In that order!)

» Role-Play: The most effective way to practice

CHAPTER 7

. . . .

THE CUSTOMER EXPERIENCE REVOLUTION

"Profit in business comes from repeat customers, customers that boast about your project or service, and customers that bring friends with them."

W. Edwards Deming

As a kid, I was told about the Golden Rule: *Do unto others as you would have them do unto you.* For many generations, this was considered the standard for treating people with respect, and many companies still follow this rule today when it comes to customer service. Unfortunately, the Golden Rule is stuck in the past and doesn't align well with today's customer experience revolution. People are not all alike and we shouldn't assume they want the same things as we do. That's why I encourage you to focus on the Platinum Rule: *Do unto others as they would want done to them.* This makes service about the client, not about you. That's real service.

This year, 89 percent of companies are expecting to compete for business primarily based on the customer experience they provide. This has rapidly increased from only 36 percent in 2011.[16] Companies know that offering the lowest price isn't going to result in the highest sales.

Providing the highest level of quality isn't going to do it either. Instead, they know they have to create a better *experience* for customers than anyone else. As a salesperson, instead of just facilitating a transaction where you help customers purchase something they want and/or need, you have to make sure customers like working with you and your company. It has to be enjoyable.

You may be thinking that this is nothing new; making customers like you has always been paramount to being in sales. Salespeople have always needed to show their personality and build relationships. While this has always been true, the bar has just gotten a little higher.

There are a variety of factors that have transformed the customer experience over the years, but one of the most important is the sheer number of purchasing options available to consumers for just about anything they want to buy. For example, people used to buy groceries from their local farmer's market or grocery store. If they weren't pleased with the selection or service, too bad. They still had to eat. Sure, they could drive to a store that's farther away, but it's a hassle and the store might not be any better. Today, there are tons of options for purchasing food. Big-box grocery stores carry popular brands, specialty stores have imported products and lots of organic food, and wholesale club stores pass on bulk discounts. People can also get their groceries delivered through online services like Peapod or Amazon. Or they can choose not to buy groceries at all and instead go to one of the many restaurants in the area or have a restaurant deliver food. If customers have a bad experience at one of those businesses, there are a variety of competitors to try next time.

With all of the choices available today, we've become accustomed to getting what we want pretty much all of the time. And yes, we want it all. From banking to baby food and everything in between, our purchasing possibilities are seemingly endless. As customers, that means we have power. Businesses will bend over backward to get our purchasing dollars, and we know it. It sure is nice to be a consumer! But wait—this book is about selling, not buying. In that case, we have some work to do.

Some people say that customers today have become entitled, but in reality, they just know what they can get. This transformation is making the sales role even more complex. We need to adjust our approach for today's prospects and customers who want it all and step up the experience we provide. In fact, sometimes the customer experience is the only thing we can control. Depending on what we sell, sometimes we can affect the quality or price, but other times that's out of our hands. (We can relay customer feedback to our boss that the new laptops we sell have problems with the touchpad, but we can't fix it directly. Along the same lines, we can tell our company that the price point for the new laptops seems a bit high, but we might not be able to offer a deal to customers.) Although those two important elements—price and quality— aren't always in our control, the experience we provide customers *is* within our control. We are empowered to cater to customers in the sales process and stand out by creating a superior experience.

Whether you sell something that only requires a one-time interaction or you support current clients on an ongoing basis, you need to be thinking about how you can improve the customer experience. This is an area where you have to push yourself. Chances are, there's no one monitoring all of your interactions with clients to see if you contact people often enough or in the right ways. If you work from home, you might not have supervision at all. Or if you own your own business, everything is up to your discretion. That means it's all on you to stay motivated. After all, great service isn't just doing what you are supposed to do. It's about going above and beyond to make people feel good about their purchase and good about working with you.

PLAY BOX CASE STUDY: HAVE A PLAN

My friend Bob Maunsell owns Electronic Security Group, and he places a high value on maintaining positive relationships with customers. After he sells a security system to a business or homeowner, that's when his work really starts. His team monitors the systems 24/7, but they would typically only need to speak with customers if something goes wrong. However, Bob decided that he wants to communicate with customers on an ongoing basis and show how much the company values their business. That's why Bob developed a plan to provide a top-notch experience from the prospecting phase all the way through long-term customer relationships.

Although Bob uses a variety of methods to connect with established customers, he says that using the phone is the best for prospecting. He can quickly get to know prospects on a more personal level over the phone, which results in a lot of success in building relationships with new people. And after he brings on a new client, he makes sure he stays connected. Bob developed a program where new customers receive three different gifts three weeks in a row. He typically sends a thank you card, a small gift certificate, and some type of baked good like Grandma's Coffee Cake. This puts a positive spin on the relationship from the very beginning. Bob also sends a monthly e-newsletter to all customers to share any updates about the company and helpful tips on keeping their office, business, and home secure. Customers also get a personal follow-up from Bob on their one-year anniversary of working with his company. Considering Bob's hard work maintaining relationships with customers, it's no surprise that he's retained many accounts for more than 20 years, many of which became clients as the result of a prospecting call.

Why is Bob so effective at producing an excellent customer experience? It's the combination of knowing that customer relationships need to be maintained, and developing a system for doing it well every single time. The system aspect is where salespeople usually get tripped up, so that's what we're going to focus on next.

DEVELOPING A COMMUNICATION SYSTEM

The cornerstone of customer experience is communication. People want to know what's going on. They want to know you haven't forgotten about them. Whether you work with the same customers on an ongoing basis or you sell one-off products and services, communication is crucial for supporting a steady stream of revenue. In real estate it was pretty common for people to say they never heard from their agents, especially when the home was not selling. Many agents will avoid calling the sellers because they did not know how to deal with the bad news. The problem with this is your customer is wondering what is going on and ultimately thinks you don't care. Personally, I feel this is another form of call reluctance. Reluctance to deal with a difficult conversation.

All too often, salespeople wait until a contract is coming to an end to reach out to a customer and try to renew or retain their business. I'm embarrassed to admit that before I started focusing on service I had many clients say, "The only times we heard from you were when you wanted a price reduction and now when our contract is up. We're all set!" It's a logical reaction, right? If you haven't talked to customers in forever, why would they want to keep working with you? You haven't put in the time to make sure they are happy with your product or service. Even if they are relatively satisfied, without a strong relationship, they are unlikely to feel loyal. That means they could be easily persuaded by a better deal or another salesperson who is more attentive to their needs. That's why you need to keep in touch and check in every once in a while even if you don't have any news. The way to do this is to have a system.

There are a variety of reasons why salespeople don't contact current customers as often as they should. The primary reasons are time management and the drive to go after the next sale. As salespeople we are busy selling, busy finding new clients and meeting our quotas. It's not that we are ignoring our clients—we just get distracted by other tasks. Relationships that seem to be sailing along aren't always at the top of your list of priorities, right? But pretty soon, day after day of not making something a priority can make a good thing turn bad. It's kind of like going to the gym every day and finally achieving the perfect abs you've always wanted, and then thinking your work is over. When working on your abs is no longer a priority, of course they're gone before you know it.

When you work hard to get something you want, whether it's great abs or a great client, you owe it to yourself to put in the work to maintain it. Maintaining something is almost always easier than starting from scratch. (e.g., repeat sales and upsells vs. closing a new customer.) Your best option for maintaining positive relationships is to develop a good system for staying on track and organized.

PLAY BOX EXERCISE: SET YOUR COMMUNICATION FREQUENCY

Stop and think about how often you think you should be connecting with customers. If you manage ongoing accounts, maybe you need to talk to customers a few times a week or even every day. Or maybe your work supporting customers is technically finished after you make the sale, but you want to stay in touch and connect with them once or twice a

---

year. Whatever the frequency, write it down. If it's different timelines for different clients, that's fine. Write down a number for each account you manage.

_____

_____

_____

_____

Next, make a plan to talk to your customers that often. (Or if you already had a plan, check to see if you're following through with it or if you've accidentally slacked off.) Set reminders for yourself or time block your calendar. This will help you if you sometimes procrastinate checking in with customers. You've set a concrete plan to hold yourself accountable, which means you'll be well aware when you get off track. Later in the book, we will cover a variety of methods for following up with customers per the timeline you set.

TIME MANAGEMENT

With all of the frequent communicating you're going to be doing, you'll need to be efficient so that you don't run out of hours in the day. The good thing about the phone is that a quick conversation is often more efficient than writing an email. However, sometimes it's hard to quickly check in with customers who are social or always have a lot of non-urgent questions. You want to connect with them and make sure they know you're available to help, but your schedule is probably packed and you have a lot of competing priorities. Don't let the fear of spending too much time on the phone keep you from checking in regularly. Try some of the following Play call tips for time management on calls:

» Set expectations upfront on the length of the call, and stick to that timeframe. If you're putting it on the calendar and sending the client an invite, schedule the call for however long you think you'll need. Depending on what you sell and what you need to discuss, you might need to talk for just a couple of minutes, or it could be much longer. Either way, make sure you're on the same page with the customer at the beginning of the call. If you prefer to make impromptu calls, say at the beginning that you only have a few minutes to talk, or that you have a hard stop at a specific time. You can also frame it in a way that is respectful of the client's time. I usually say something like, "Hey, do you have a few minutes? I just wanted to share some quick information with you. I know you're busy so I won't keep you."

» Leave voicemails. If your client doesn't answer, don't hang up. A voice message can be an effective way to communicate whatever you need to share. You can ask them to call you back only if they need more info. Your High D client will certainly appreciate this. And let's be honest—sometimes you call clients and you hope they won't pick up. Maybe because you don't have time for a longer call or you aren't ready to answer additional questions they might have. But a voicemail can be quicker for you than writing an email and you can still convey personality and tone. Luckily, there's a service called slydial you can use to make calls that bypass the phone ringing and go straight to voicemail. The person receiving the message shouldn't know you did something to intentionally go straight to voicemail, especially since cellphones do that a lot of times anyway. Don't get me wrong; I'm not advocating this as a way to avoid clients. But the reality is that sometimes you will be incredibly short on time. If the choice is between not following up that day and intentionally going straight to voicemail to share a brief message, communicating more often is the better option. It can also be especially good for customers who don't check email that often and prefer to get information over the phone.

QUALITY INTERACTIONS

We've discussed the importance of the quantity and efficiency of the interactions you have with customers, but don't forget about the quality. We're usually on top of our game when we're prospecting, but when we work with accounts on an ongoing basis it can be more challenging. Over time, it's sometimes easy to think of these relationships as casual and the interactions as less important. Instead of always being on point, we tend to relax a little.

For example, instead of being 10 minutes early to meetings, maybe you're a minute or two late. (He'll understand!) Or you went from dressing professionally to wearing jeans and sneakers sometimes. (She seems OK with being casual!) Or somewhere along the way you stopped emailing an agenda of discussion points before calls. (Maybe he never reads it anyway!) Let's stop right here. Even when you know clients well, they will never be like regular co-workers. Sure, you can let your guard down a little and loosen up, but don't forget who's paying you. Even though you've secured agreements with customers or have ongoing work orders doesn't mean they are obligated to stay with you forever. You've won their current business but not necessarily their future business. When it comes to customers' expectations today, the bar is constantly being raised. And as long as businesses continue to step up to the plate and provide better and better service, I don't see this trend stopping anytime soon. The fact is, there are plenty of other salespeople out there who work for your competitors and they are hungry to drum up new business. If your customers got a call from one of those salespeople, how easy do you think it would be to close them? If you've provided an excellent experience, you stand a much better chance of earning their loyalty. Here are some helpful tips for elevating the quality of your communication:

» Make your interactions with customers about them, not you. Ask how they're doing and get to know them. Let them do most of the talking and continue taking notes on what they say. If they are taking a vacation or planning a kid's birthday party next weekend, write it down and ask about it later. Even if you've already won their business, show you are listening and that you still care.

» Ask prospects and current customers how they like to be contacted. Do they prefer to talk on the phone, send texts, communicate via email, or message through social media? You may think one method is easiest, but people are different. Don't assume—ask.

» Anticipate customers' wants and needs and go out of your way to address them. A real estate agent friend of mine does a great job of this, and it truly sets him apart from his competitors. He owns a moving truck that he lets his clients use so it's one less thing for them to worry about or pay for. And on their first night in a new home, he always buys his customers a nice dinner so they don't have to cook. Little things like that go a long way to show he understands his customers.

» Ask current customers for feedback so you know what they value about your company and what you could do better. This shows you care about the product and service you are providing and want them to have a good experience. You can ask for feedback informally over the phone or send a quick note to customers. If your company doesn't send customer feedback surveys, suggest it to your manager.

» Use a system for getting feedback regularly. In my real estate business the goal is to call our clients every Monday just to check in so they knew we did not forget about them. Some clients would tell us that there is no need to call weekly but we would leave that for them to decide. We also use a customer survey so people can give anonymous feedback. We send it out after 30 days of working together, and again after 90 days. If you have a smaller business or budget, free tools like Survey Monkey can be great.

PLAY BOX CASE STUDY: TRACKING CUSTOMER INTERACTIONS

Flannery works for an information technology company that supplies small and large businesses with IT equipment and support. Salespeople at her company have an average of 60-90 accounts that they sell to on an ongoing basis, all the while maintaining relationships and making sure customers have a positive experience. That's no small feat for Flannery, especially because all of her customers have different contracts and they are on difference sales cycles. Some are in the process of upgrading their entire corporation's computer infrastructure, while others are buying a laptop one-off here and there. Keeping up with all of her clients' individual needs and timelines can be challenging. Bigger projects can easily become a current focus and major time commitment, but she can't forget about other accounts in the meantime.

Luckily, Flannery's company has developed its own CRM system that has the functionality salespeople need to stay organized. The system links to salespeople's phones and tracks calls. It automatically matches phone numbers to contacts in the database and populates the call history for all accounts. This functionality saves salespeople time because they don't

---

have to manually track their calls. When Flannery looks up a customer in the system, she can quickly and easily see all of the dates she's spoken to them and how long each call lasted.

The system also serves as a tool for the company to monitor salespeople's work habits because it tracks the total amount of time spent on the phone. Managers know that when salespeople spend time talking with customers on a regular basis, they provide better support, which drives stronger relationships. It is also more likely that salespeople will learn about any additional IT needs that customers may have and be able to offer other solutions, which translates into more sales. For these reasons, the company encourages salespeople to talk on the phone. In fact, they set quotas for total time on the phone based on the salesperson's level within the company. Although managers don't typically review the details of who salespeople call and how long they talk, the total time shows whether salespeople are doing a good job staying in contact with their accounts.

Flannery says that the tracking system changes the way she and her co-workers approach interacting with customers. Since they are held accountable for spending a lot of time on the phone, they don't hesitate to call customers. Picking up the phone is essential for meeting their performance goals, so they do it from the very beginning of working with the company. And in doing so, salespeople learn that their managers are right—it actually is common to hear about additional IT needs when they talk to customers directly. Calling customers frequently helps them sell more than they originally anticipated.[17]

As an IT supplier would know, technology makes things easier. This particular CRM system saves salespeople time, helps them stay organized, ultimately helps them sell more, and serves as a valuable tool for managers to monitor their team's performance. Getting a system like this in place is certainly a best practice for any sales organization.

HANDLING PROBLEMS

It would be great if we were always able to provide a perfect experience for our customers, but sometimes things go wrong. The way we handle mistakes can either make a situation much worse and lose a customer for good, or reinforce that hiring us was the right choice.

When things go wrong, accountability and responsibility are extremely important. Customers want to know that we acknowledge the mistake, and just like them, find it unacceptable. This is such a simple piece of advice, yet many salespeople come up short here. Instead of stepping up and taking responsibility, sometimes salespeople try to downplay mistakes or brush them under the rug altogether. When this happens, it's basically like assuming the customer is stupid. It might sound insulting to describe it this way, but it feels just as insulting to be treated this way. Customers aren't stupid. They notice when they aren't receiving what they signed up for. When we fail to acknowledge that we messed up or over-promised, we can pretty much kiss the relationship goodbye. On the flip side, when we take accountability and act quickly to resolve an issue, we seize the opportunity to create a raving fan.

When things go wrong, the best thing you can do is pick up the phone and talk to customers directly and immediately, the sooner the better. This will make it easier to show your sincerity and respond to their concerns in real time. Don't forget that customer service is about serving. You need to stay humble and remember that your role is to help. When you approach customer interactions with this mindset, you'll be well positioned to provide a great experience working with your company.

LEAVE LASTING IMPRESSIONS

When your relationships with clients are not ongoing, you always want to end projects on a positive note. This helps clients remember how much they enjoyed working with you. You never know if they will need the same product or service again or they'll be in a position to refer you to someone they know.

My friend recently got married and had the challenging experience of planning a destination wedding and hiring vendors she couldn't meet in person. After speaking with a few photographers over the phone, she and her husband chose a small business owner and photographer named Gabby, primarily because they liked her. Gabby had beautiful pictures and great online reviews, but so did all of the other photographers they considered. They thought Gabby seemed like she would be nice to work with, and as it turns out, they were right. Gabby provided an excellent experience from start to finish, and she was especially clever in how she made sure a good impression stuck with the bride and groom.

After the wedding, Gabby sent low-resolution images well ahead of the agreed-upon deadline. When she followed up later with the high-resolution image CD, she again went a step beyond what was expected. Instead of just popping the disk in an envelope like the couple expected, she sent them a care package. She printed not one, but three small photo collections that were ready for display, one for the bride and groom and one for both sets of parents. She also sent a bonus flash drive, and wrapped everything up in printed cloth and twine. Even though their relationship was technically over and Gabby had already been paid, the package served as a reminder of what a great experience it was working with her. A few weeks later when the bride was asked for recommendations for wedding vendors, who do you think was at the top of her list?

MANAGING UNHEALTHY RELATIONSHIPS

As a salesperson, you will probably get used to talking to cranky people on the phone, but you need to be aware of when attitudes cross the line. Everyone can have a bad day, but there is a difference between an isolated incident and reoccurring abuse. I interviewed Kevin Sheridan, a serial entrepreneur and the former founder and CEO of HR Solutions, who learned how to manage negative client relationships through experience. Over the 18 years he managed the consulting firm, Sheridan was always very focused on driving sales and growing the company, but he quickly realized how detrimental it is to bring in the wrong kind of new business.

Sometimes clients who seemed perfectly nice in the beginning turned out to be tyrants and Sheridan's account managers had to deal with verbal abuse. They would spend a good deal of time talking to clients on the phone every day, sometimes being berated or belittled on a regular basis. Sheridan wasn't comfortable subjecting his employees to that kind of treatment, so when clients became a problem, his team would have a meeting. They would discuss whether they should fire the client or at the next opportunity change the project pricing to include a "PITA" (Pain in the Ass) premium. Sheridan would give 50 percent of the PITA fee to the employees who managed the client relationship, and the employees had a say in whether it was worth charging more or if the client should be let go.

When the choice was to fire the client, they would do it professionally, saying something like, "We think you would be better served by another vendor. This doesn't feel like a positive partnership, and we want you to be happy." Sheridan says clients were not surprised when it would come to this. Over 18 years, Sheridan fired about 15 clients, including a $900,000 annual contract with a bank where the point person ended up being especially nasty.[18]

As a salesperson and/or entrepreneur, it's hard to turn down business, but it's also important to see the big picture. When you play not to lose clients, you sacrifice your employees' well being. Sometimes people get angry and say things over the phone that they wouldn't have the nerve to say in person. Upholding relationships where clients consistently do this just isn't worth it, especially when there are many other prospects out there you could be going after instead.

SUMMARY

Thinking back to the beginning of my sales career, I cannot think of one single company, with the exception of Keller Williams, that trained salespeople on customer service, let alone customer experience. I don't mean to discount any of the other companies I worked for. I think they were following industry norms over the years. It seems like everyone is just now catching up to realizing that we have to take better care of our customers. The one thing I learned from years and years of chasing new business and almost burning out multiple times, is that it's easier and costs less to keep your existing business than to drum up new customers. The key to success in business is keeping existing customers happy!

Whether you sell one-off products or services or you've been working with mostly the same clients for 50 years, providing a top-notch experience needs to be your priority. It will set you apart from competitors, build loyalty, and take your career to the next level. Remember, the customer experience isn't a destination you reach. It's an ongoing journey.

KEY TAKEAWAYS:

» Develop a communication system: know how often you should contact customers

» Track your outreach: it should be easy to reference your interactions with customers

» Cater to customers: make interactions about them, not you

» Get feedback from clients

» Get reviews and testimonials

CHAPTER 8

· · · · · · · · · ·

STOP TELLING AND START LISTENING

*"You can have everything in life you want, if you will just help
enough other people get what they want."*

Zig Ziglar [19]

Have you ever noticed how some people you meet are instantly
likeable? It's easy to talk to them, the conversation flows well, and
you let your guard down. Instead of worrying what they think, you open
up as if you were talking to an old friend.

There are many factors that contribute to likeability, but one of the
biggest is feeling as though the other person is genuinely interested in
you. How do some people project interest and caring in others while
some people don't? It's simple: instead of talking about themselves, they
ask you questions about yourself. They win you over by listening. As
salespeople, this is what we need to do when we talk with prospects.

It's scientifically proven that people like talking about themselves.
Harvard neuroscience researchers Diana Tamir and Jason Mitchell
found that our brains find self-disclosure "extra rewarding." When
people talk about themselves, the brain triggers the same pleasure
centers it does with food and money. It's believed that this is one reason
why sharing on social media has become so popular. Whether online or

in personal conversation, people feel a rush of pleasure when they tell others about their lives.

As a salesperson, it's incredibly important to understand how this scientific finding affects our conversations. You might have the urge to tell prospects all of the great things your company does and the many reasons they should buy your product, but that creates a one-sided conversation that makes *you* feel good. To be a successful salesperson, you need to master the art of making the *other person* feel good, (e.g., important) during conversations. This starts with asking great questions that encourage your prospects to talk about themselves, their challenges, what they want, or even better, their Big Why and motivation.

I once heard John Maxwell say: "People don't care how much you know until they know how much you care."

Asking the right questions and uncovering real motivation shows you care. And when prospects can tell you care about them, they are much more likely to trust you and buy from you. Additionally, something interesting happens when you actually stop and listen to people. You get to know them and you really will start to care about them as individuals. You'll learn about their pain points and motivators, and you can be empathetic to their unique situations. As it turns out, empathy is sometimes considered the number one quality in an effective sales message. Darren Hardy, author of *The Entrepreneurial Roller Coaster*, says empathy allows salespeople to connect with customers on a gut level.[20] Keep this in mind when you make your calls.

While I was writing this book, a lot of people told me about their experiences talking with salespeople over the phone. It was shocking to me how often potential customers are on the verge of buying something but the salesperson blows it by not picking up on obvious clues. My friend Mia is a great example of this. She had a couple of IRA and 401K retirement accounts held by different investment companies that were chosen by her past employers. For simplicity, she wanted to transfer them all into one investment company. When stopping by her bank to get a new debit card, she asked if the bank could help her with that. She was introduced to one of their financial advisors (who are responsible for bringing in new business), but she was on her lunch break and didn't have time to talk. The advisor got Mia's number and said he would call her to follow up. She ended up making an appointment to meet with him but had to cancel it at the last minute because she had to travel for work. He called her back to reschedule, but Mia's calendar was completely booked for the next couple of weeks. She told him she was still interested in working with him but that she was extremely busy and overwhelmed with work, and just couldn't commit to another meeting at this point. She said she hoped to think about switching her investments within the next month or two when things calmed down. The financial advisor decided to take this opportunity to spend the next 10 minutes babbling about how great he is at his job, how great his company is, and why it's so important that Mia work with them. This was directly after Mia said she was busy and overwhelmed! There weren't any nuances to pick up on here—the guy just didn't listen to her. Plain and simple. (Honestly, I think the only reason she stayed on the phone is because she knew I was writing this book and wanted to help with a little field research!) When the advisor finally wrapped up his spiel, Mia felt like he didn't care about her at all. He had done all of the talking, and he made it all about him and his company. On top of that, he didn't respect the one thing she said was important to her at the moment: her time.

A few months later, Mia followed through and transferred her retirement accounts, but she went through a different bank. This story is an excellent example of what happens when you don't listen. You close the door on getting to know prospects and understanding their needs. You can also totally blow it without knowing why. The advisor called

Mia later to follow up, but she didn't pick up. Obviously he didn't realize what a buffoon he was on their last call.

This brings up another good point: not all prospects feel comfortable asserting themselves or hanging up when a salesperson is talking their ear off. Just because someone hasn't cut you off yet doesn't mean you should keep talking. So how do you know when you've said enough? I advise that you follow a general rule.

THE 70/30 RULE

As a guide for how much talking and listening you should do when calling a prospect, I follow the 70/30 rule: Listen 70 percent of the time and talk 30 percent of the time. Of course conversations will vary depending on what you sell, the stage in the sales funnel, and whether your prospect is introverted or extroverted, but aiming for listening 70 percent of the time is a good goal. In any situation, you shouldn't do more than 50 percent of the talking. If that sounds difficult or even impossible, don't worry! This chapter will show you helpful techniques for asking insightful questions and getting prospects to open up.

PLAY BOX EXERCISE: HOW MUCH DO YOU LISTEN?

To improve on something you have to know where you currently stand. What percent of your conversations with prospects are spent listening? Don't guess off the top of your head because it's unlikely to be accurate. Instead, keep a notepad nearby when you make calls this week and jot down your estimate after every call. Be honest even if you aren't happy with your estimate. At the end of the week, calculate your average and write it down in the following space.

_____

_____

_____

A great way to gauge this is to count the number of questions you asked and the number of statements you made. These numbers won't lie. You could also ask for permission to record your sales calls. Listening to yourself after a call is the best way to evaluate how well you listened during the call.

HOW TO ASK QUESTIONS

Do you ever watch late-night TV and think about what a great job the hosts have? Guys like Jimmy Fallon and Jimmy Kimmel make it look so easy. They just sit at their desks, as cool as cucumbers, always knowing what to ask to get all kinds of celebrities to open up. They always seem fully in control of the conversation and they're never at a loss for words. They make asking questions look easy, but it can be really tough! In fact, I would go so far as to say that asking questions is an art, especially when you combine it with listening, quickly processing what you hear, responding appropriately, and asking another question that moves the conversation forward. (No wonder Fallon and Kimmel get paid so well!)

To take your career to the next level, you need to hone your skills creating great questions to get your prospects to open up.

TYPES OF QUESTIONS

There are a variety of types of questions you can (and should) ask prospects. I find it helpful to organize them into groups to better formulate a strategy. All questions fall into one of the two categories below:

» **Closed-ended Questions:** Responses are limited to a list of choices and don't call for additional information. (For example, yes or no questions, or multiple-choice questions.) These types of questions are great for quickly gaining basic information, but they leave a lot unsaid.

» **Open-ended Questions:** Exploratory in nature, these questions call for longer responses. (For example, many questions beginning with "what" or "how.") These types of questions are great for getting to know prospects, when they have the time and patience to answer them.

Aside from distinguishing between open and closed-ended questions, we can divide questions by the purpose they serve:

» **Rapport Building Questions:** Help you connect personally and emotionally with prospects.

   » You were headed to your son's soccer game the last time we talked. How did it go?

   » What can I do to help you the most?

» **Fact-finding Questions:** Gather information quickly and logically.

   » Are you currently in a contract with another vendor?

   » Why are you considering switching?

» **Extension Questions:** Explore topics further.

   » Can you tell me more about that situation?

   » You mentioned efficiency being a major goal for your company with this project. Can you talk a little more about any other goals you have?

» **Emotional Questions:** Focus on how people feel and help you understand what's important to them.

   » How did you feel when that happened?

> » How would you feel if we were able to find a solution that meets all of your requirements?

The goal is to use a combination of all types of questions to create a fluid conversation where you listen, respond, and ask another question that keeps moving the discussion forward.

That said, you can't ignore the fact that asking a lot of questions can be asking a lot from prospects, especially if they weren't even planning on talking to you in the first place. Sometimes prospects will be rubbed the wrong way by your questions. They might say, "Why do you need to know all of this stuff?" or "What's with all the questions?" You can also hear in their tone of voice when they are losing patience or their guard starts to go up. When this happens, one of two things is occurring:

> » They are the problem (e.g., they aren't highly motivated to purchase)

> » You are the problem (e.g., your questions felt like an interrogation rather than a conversation)

When prospects aren't motivated to purchase, you should move on. Add them to your database so they get your emails and consider putting them in the long-term follow up list.

On the flip side, if prospects aren't opening up because of how you're asking questions, you need to step it up and do a better job of guiding the conversation and making it clear why you need various answers. In addition to asking questions, make sure you're framing them in a way that explains how the answers will help you provide better service. I always say something like, "My goal is to help you achieve your goals. To do that, I need to have a better understanding of what's important to you. Can you tell me more about XYZ?" This will help reinforce how you're on your prospect's side.

You should also have a strategy for asking questions where one answer builds on another. An effective sequence of questions helps you understand your prospect's goals, uncover their pain points/motivation and gets them to trust you. Great questions stimulate an interesting discussion and the next question is often found in the answer to the previous question. For that reason, you have to be agile in your conversations. You can plan what questions to ask ahead of time, but know that you will most likely have to deviate from your plan, or at least adjust the order because it won't perfectly align with the natural flow of your conversation. You must be present and listen to prospects' answers, instead of using that time to focus on the next question you're going to ask. It's easy to hold back and not talk for 70 percent of your interactions, but it's much harder to convert that time into quality listening. Successfully doing so can be the difference-maker between leading an interesting conversation that encourages prospects to open up and peppering questions in a way that feels like an interrogation. And no one likes to be interrogated.

UNCOVER MOTIVATION

In addition to making prospects more inclined to like and trust you, letting them do the talking serves another extremely important purpose: you don't know why people would buy what you're selling unless you know at least a little about their motivation. What looks like a no-brainer benefit to you might be irrelevant to them. Or worse, what you suggest as a benefit might actually discourage someone from buying. Not everyone wants the newest thing on the market or the least expensive option. Not everyone cares how much research your company invests in or how much customer support you offer. People are different, their situations are different, and they view the world in different ways. Instead of assuming you know what motivates prospects to buy, you need to find out. The best way to find out is by asking great questions and truly listening to the answers.

I've coached a lot of salespeople over the years and one of the most important things I teach is how to ask the right questions to find out what a prospect really wants. For example, in real estate, prospects want to sell their homes. Some salespeople think that's the motivational factor right there—selling the home. But that's just the surface. The real motivation is deeper.

When I call prospects, no matter whether I know them personally or I've never spoken to them before, I don't make any assumptions about why they are selling. The first thing I usually ask is, "Why are you selling your house?" For me, this helps remove any of my biases. From the way people are sometimes taken aback by this simple question I can tell that even if they've spoken with other realtors, many have never been asked this question before.

Suppose I call a prospect, Mrs. Brandt, and ask her my opening question. She says that she and her husband are selling their home because they want to move to Florida. Again, I could stop there and make an assumption why Mrs. Brandt wants to sell. She lives in Boston and Florida is obviously much warmer, without the terrible winters we often have. Plus she sounds like she could be near retirement age and I know Florida is a popular retirement destination. However, if I were to assume that's why she wants to sell her house I'd be going on limited information and a stereotype. That wouldn't be smart because there's a big chance I could be wrong.

To dig deeper, I might say something like, "Yeah, Florida is a nice place! What part of Florida?" When she answers, I could say something positive about that area and then ask what is bringing her to Florida. I may also ask her to tell me what's the most important thing about the move. It sounds like I'm making casual conversation, but I'm actually getting closer to the root of her motivation. In this case, let's say Mrs. Brandt replies that she and her husband's children and grandchildren live in Florida. Bingo! The Brandts want to be closer to their grandchildren. That's what they *really* want. From that point forward, I know that to relate to Mrs. Brandt on a personal level, I need to show how I can help her reach her goal of being closer to her grandchildren and how I can do it better than my competitors. In this case, better might mean faster, but again, that would be an assumption. Instead of guessing, I can use the strategy of "going three deep" with my motivational questions. Asking three questions about motivation that all build on each other helps to get to the root of a prospect's motivation. I can ask Mrs. Brandt what she's most looking forward to in living near her children and grandchildren. No matter what she says, I will gain a better understanding of how she's thinking, and I might also learn other related motivational factors. For example, if she says that she doesn't want to miss holidays or milestones in their lives, I know that she has a sense of urgency to make a decision. I know that a good angle to take with this prospect is sharing how quickly I expect to sell her home and how pricing would effect their goals. But then I wouldn't stop there. I would ask what would happen if they didn't move and then I would get the real answer. Her children are actually moving her down to Florida so they can watch over her as she gets older and she is having some health issues, plus I just learned that the children also need to be included in the decision making process.

Let's back up here and rehash how far I've come with just a few questions. At the beginning of the call, I didn't even know why Mrs. Brandt wanted to sell her house. I also didn't know what could motivate her to choose me as her realtor. Without that knowledge, I could have given her a general sales presentation and shared the top selling points as I see them, but it probably wouldn't have been very enticing, plus she may not have even been able to hire me without consulting her kids first. With just a few questions I learned a lot and I asked the questions in a way that was natural, conversational, and allowed Mrs. Brandt to talk about what was really important about the move. From my experience at KW, most of our competitors do not go as deep as we do with questions, and they lose a lot of business to us because of it.

This strategy transfers over to all industries and works for B to B and B to C. Remember that in order to effectively tailor your sale presentation to your prospects, you have to understand their motivation. No matter what you sell, this understanding stems from the art of asking the right questions and truly listening to the answers.

THE BENEFIT AND

Thinking back to my prospect Mrs. Brandt and how she wants to sell her home quickly, I am eager to tell her how I am one of the top-ranking relators in my company. In my mind, this shows that I'm the best guy for the job. However, to Mrs. Brandt who is likely unfamiliar with my industry, this could just sound like bragging. Or it might have no significance to her whatsoever. Why would she care that I am one of the top-ranking realtors? She isn't invested in my professional success. She just wants to know what I can do for her. Instead of just sharing a selling point, I need to explain why it's relevant.

This is what I call the benefit AND approach. In this case, it would go something like this: "I am one of the top-ranking realtors in my company, which means I have a lot of experience selling homes at prices that met the sellers' goals. For you, Mrs. Brandt, this means that you would have confidence and peace of mind that your home would sell quickly at the best price out there."

See how much more enticing that is than if I were to just say I'm a top realtor? As salespeople, we get so used to the selling points we share in presentations that it can be hard to take a step back and try to hear the information like it's brand new. The best thing you can do is to put yourself in your prospect's shoes and think: So what? Who cares? What about me?

After you share your benefit AND, you should always ask prospects how they feel about the information you just shared. Remember, you don't want to do all the talking, and it helps to get feedback from prospects on whether they are motivated by the points you've mentioned. (You can also see how this strategy would have helped the financial advisor better relate to my friend Mia.)

PLAY BOX EXERCISE: IDENTIFY YOUR BENEFIT AND

I bet your wheels are already turning thinking about how you share benefits in your presentations. Maybe you already follow this format or maybe it's totally new to you. In either case, it's helpful to brainstorm on how the benefits you offer will make a real difference in your customers' lives.

Write down three benefits of working with you and/or your company. Next, write down at least three reasons why customers should care. What's in it for them?

_____

_____

_____

Once you've identified how your selling points directly impact customers, it will be easier to tie them to the motivational factors you uncover while asking questions.

BECOMING A BETTER LISTENER

As a society, we have become less engaged in personal interactions than we once were. People leave their cellphones on the dinner table and send text messages in between bites—even if the person sitting right across from them is talking. That's what people think of listening today. That you can do it while doing two other things at the same time. Well, I'm here to tell you that you can't. Not well, anyway.

Like a lot of things, listening comes in a wide range of quality from terrible to superb. When you don't listen well, you don't absorb or retain much information. You might get the jest of a message, but you're tuning in and out like a radio station a few towns over. You're missing chunks of the conversation, but you aren't sure what you're missing. And because you weren't really listening, you probably didn't hear anything interesting and won't commit the conversation to memory. On the flip side, when you do an excellent job of listening, you hear all of the words being said, but you're empowered to hear even more. The hesitation in someone's voice; the excitement when a prospect talks about her goals; the basketball game on TV in the background; the subtle hint of a southern accent. All of these small details come together to paint a larger picture, but only if you take the time and effort to notice them. The better you are at listening the better you will be at selling. Pure and simple.

Here are some tips for becoming a better listener:

Remove distractions: All kinds of things can derail your concentration. You should do your best to eliminate anything that could be distracting, even if it means logging out of your email for short periods of time. If you work from home, be aware that you have even more temptations to distract you, especially if other family members or roommates are home. Do your best to find a quiet spot.

Take notes: We've talked about the importance of taking notes for organizational purposes, but it also helps you stay concentrated and engaged in conversations. If prospects go on tangents, don't let your mind drift. Instead, you can take notes on their personality type or other impressions you're getting from the call.

Stop focusing on what you're going to say next: When your mind is in two places, you won't be as good at listening. A great example of this is when you meet new people and don't remember their name. It's probably because you never heard it in the first place because you were thinking too hard about saying your own name and making a good first impression. When you hear people talk about being present, this is what they are talking about; being in the moment instead of being lost in your own thoughts. The most effective way to be present and stop worrying about what you're going to say next is to get more comfortable on the phone. Practice your scripts, role-play, and take a moment to calm your mind. Then make the call to your prospect or client.

Try harder outside of work too: Prospects aren't the only people who value your undivided attention. Your family and friends want to know you're listening and you care about them too. If you try harder to become a better listener in your personal relationships, your good habits will carry over into your professional life.

When you become a better listener, you will find yourself genuinely interested in people more often than you were in the past. It will seem like the world has turned into a more interesting place, but it's actually you becoming more aware of the nuances that surround you. Probably the greatest benefit of listening better is that people will become more interesting to you.

OVERCOMING OBJECTIONS: THE AEIIOU APPROACH

Even when you're a great listener, prospects aren't always forthright with their objections. But if you don't know what's holding people back, you can't effectively sell to them. That's why you sometimes need to make an extra effort to understand where prospects are coming from.

Objections typically come up in the beginning of the sales cycle and at the end. After you get past initial objections and present your information, your prospect is then faced with the decision to purchase. That's when new objections surface and old objections resurface. When this happens, don't get discouraged. Objections show that prospects are interested enough in working with you to consider what you're offering. If they weren't interested, they wouldn't continue to give you the time of day. Adjust your mindset to think of objections as progress. But it's important for you to understand these objections so that you can discuss them and get past them.

When I'm close to closing a prospect, I find it helpful to use the AEIIOU approach. I was first taught this model when I became a KW University instructor, but I've adapted it over the years.

- » **Ask:** Sometimes real objections are hidden under other objections. Ask a question relating to the objection to get to the heart of the issue. (e.g., "Can you tell me more about that?" or "Can you tell me what's important about that?")
- » **Empathize:** Acknowledge their concern and show you care.
- » **Identify:** Restate what you believe the real issue is, just to be sure.
- » **Isolate:** Figure out if this is the only objection stopping them from deciding to hire you today.
- » **Offer a solution:** Explain how you can help them overcome their objection.
- » **Urge an agreement:** Go for the close.

Here's an example of AEIIOU in action:

Objection:

Prospect: "We're worried about the cost of this leadership development consulting package."

Ask:

Salesperson: "Can you tell me more about that?

Prospect: "Yes. We only budgeted $20,000 for leadership development. If we spend more than that, our HR team won't have as much for other talent management projects."

Empathize:

Salesperson: "I certainly understand that. You don't want to improve one program and leave another hanging by the wayside."

Identify:

Salesperson: "Just to be clear, you're saying that your team doesn't want to compromise your talent management projects for this year?"

Prospect: "Yes."

Isolate:

Salesperson: "Is that the only concern that's keeping your team from moving forward with our leadership development consulting?"

Prospect: "Yes, it's all budget issues."

Offer a solution:

Salesperson: "You mentioned before that you work with recruiters to help you find talent and that it's a burden because your turnover is high. When companies try our leadership development consulting, their voluntary turnover drops an average of 60 percent within the first three months. Leaders improve their skills so much that retention is no longer an issue. Most of our clients either stopped using recruiters altogether or they cut way back on the amount of money they spend on recruiting. So investing in leadership development would actually cut talent management costs in the long run."

Prospect: "Oh wow. That does make a difference."

Urge an agreement:

Salesperson: "Since your only concern was the budget and now you see how it won't be an issue for your HR team, it makes sense to go ahead with us, doesn't it?

Prospect: "Yes."

The AEIIOU approach works in a lot of situations, but it won't work in all situations. It really depends on the nature of the objection and whether you can offer a viable solution. Even when you can't, this approach helps you come from a place of curiosity and it frames your conversations to be about the prospect rather than yourself. Consider this another play in your sales playbook.

SUMMARY

Some people think sales is about talking—saying the right thing at the right time and magically winning others over. But sales isn't about being a smooth-talker. It's about listening. When you're a great listener, you'll be able to quickly process what you hear and respond in a thoughtful way that moves the conversation forward. Instead of relying on canned questions, your instincts will take over and you'll know exactly what to ask.

It sounds simple, but there's an art to asking the right questions. Luckily, it's something that becomes a lot easier with practice.

KEY TAKEAWAYS:

» Use the 70/30 Rule: Listen 70 percent of the time and talk 30 percent of the time

» The Benefit AND: Remember your prospect is thinking, "So what? Who cares? What about me?"

» Be present in your conversations: Listening is different from not talking

CHAPTER 9

· · · · · · · · · ·

COWBOYS VS. LIBRARIANS

"If you're not sure exactly what to do, then focus on what not to do."

Tim Ferriss

I don't know about you, but I am a huge fan of old Wild West movies. They always seem to start out with a cowboy on his horse racing into a town with guns blazing and bullets flying. Totally unintimidated by the town's bullies or corrupt officials, the cowboy overpowers whoever gets in his way, taking over the town and usually getting the girl in the end. It's exciting to watch! The cowboy's attitude and swagger have made a lot of us dream about being a cowboy ourselves. Well, movies and real life are two totally different things. The cowboy's strategy works great to get him what he wants in the Wild West, but in a modern, civilized society, this brazenness is less effective.

After establishing my prospecting company, I found myself in a position where I had to hire a team of telemarketers to help make calls and qualify leads. Since I started out in telemarketing when I was 17 years old and spent many years making cold calls, I felt confident in the system we used, and in my ability to assess applicants' skillsets and fit for the position. Whenever I would have an opening on one of my teams,

I would post job ads in the newspaper, on Craigslist, LinkedIn, Monster, and other social media sites, which typically generate a large number of applicants. I would then have all applicants do behavioral assessments, conduct the interviews and fill the positions pretty easily. Although I have talked to a ton of people over the years, I'll always remember a guy I didn't hire.

One morning I received a voicemail from a candidate named Alex, who was responding to the telemarketer job posting we ran on Craigslist. The posting we ran said, "Leave us your best voice-message explaining why we should hire you. If we are inspired, we will call you back." My thoughts on this ad were that the people who would call would be confident, which is always something we are looking for when cold calling.

I'll tell you honestly, we get dozens of messages for each job opening, and this was one of the few that was worth calling back immediately. I spoke with Alex on the phone and he seemed like a strong candidate. I was going out of town that week and needed to put the hiring process on hold, so I asked Alex to call me back in one week. As soon as I returned, I was happy to see that I had received a voicemail from him and a follow up email. Although I was interested in speaking with Alex, after being away from the office for a week, it was not my priority. I spent the morning catching up on the most pressing tasks. Around lunchtime I received another message from Alex, this time on my office phone number instead of my cell. Personally, I thought that was clever, since alternating between different numbers is a best practice for getting prospects to pick up the phone. That said, I had a lot of things that needed to get done before talking with him, so I didn't pick up. However, I was starting to become curious about Alex and I wanted to wait and see where he went from there. Around 3pm I had another missed call from the same number, and again at 4:30pm, and yet again at 6pm. This was now getting a bit annoying, but I did think, "at least he is persistent." First thing the next morning, he called again, following up with another message around 11am. Finally, at lunchtime after the ninth call, I decided to pick up the phone, mostly out of frustration and the urge to give him some candid feedback. After all, his constant phone calls were becoming disruptive and had made me not want to hire him, let alone interview him. I was frank and told Alex that what he was doing could be construed as stalking, and even though it was persistent it was not effective. Clearly offended, he said, "Well you obviously can't afford my services," and hung up.

WOW!

This guy is a great example of what I call a "Cowboy," which is one end of the behavioral spectrum in sales. Cowboys come out guns blazing, prepared for a hostile takeover. Sadly I can relate to Alex, because when I was a young salesman I did the same thing. I thought that the harder I pushed, the more likely I was to get what I wanted. I simply did not know any better. Part of the reason why I had this attitude was because I was inexperienced and somewhat immature, but another contributing factor was the training I received. I had been in sales training programs where the trainer said, "I leave the prospect with a contract in hand or in handcuffs." It sounds catchy and exciting, especially for less experienced sales professionals. Unfortunately, it's not a good sales strategy and certainly not a way to get follow up business, which is actually a key factor for long-term success.

Thinking back on this whole story makes me believe that Alex was probably trying to impress me with his persistence and follow-up skills. That's what I had been guilty of in the past—pushing and pushing until I wore people down or they got fed up. When someone said, "take me off your list," or "don't call me again," I thought the same thing as Alex; their negative reaction couldn't have been my fault. But as you know, there is a big difference between being persistent and being aggressive.

To help you understand the other end of the behavioral spectrum—the "Librarian"—consider an old colleague of mine. Like the Boy Scout motto, his goal was to "always be prepared." I would look around our office and notice how infrequently this guy was picking up the phone and talking to people compared with the rest of the sales team. I asked him if he was struggling to get people on the phone and he said no, he was just doing a little research about prospects and "doing his homework" before making the first call. I didn't say anything at the time, but his sales numbers showed that his approach wasn't working out too well. Although his intentions were good, he was spending way too much time researching unqualified leads. For example, he would spend 20 minutes collecting information about a single opportunity only to call the prospect and find out they went with a competitor last month. His Achilles heel was that he didn't feel comfortable reaching out to a prospect until he did background research on the company and ideally the decision-maker as well. Have you ever heard the saying, "paralysis by analysis"? This is the perfect example of the Librarian.

Both Cowboys and Librarians exhibit a wide variety of traits, many of which are problematic:

COWBOYS

» Go for the "wing it" approach when contacting prospects: talk first think later

» Have a tendency to over-promise, oftentimes unintentionally misleading prospects or misrepresenting service offerings

» Think the ends justify the means

» Overly aggressive

» Will say anything to get the sale

» Burn bridges and lose the opportunity to get referrals

LIBRARIANS

» Lack a sense of urgency

» Waste time over researching leads

» Can seem uninspiring or uninteresting

» Appear to have low confidence

» Underestimate how much they can help prospects

» Too timid on follow up

» Take a thoughtful approach that is not always noticed by prospects

As you can see, these are two far ends of the behavioral spectrum. Throughout my years in sales, I've come to know a lot of people on either end. Depending on the industry, being closer to one end can serve salespeople well. For example, Librarians can thrive when an extremely thoughtful approach yields a higher win percentage. (Usually the higher the price level of what you sell, the more research is needed upfront.) But in other industries, doing a lot of research wastes valuable time and there aren't enough hours in the day to win the numbers game. Cowboys thrive in short sales cycles, especially when using lead lists that haven't been vetted or prequalified.

Although the smartest approach depends on your industry, the product or service you're selling, local cultural norms, and your own personal wiring, balance is key. And when people are on one end of either spectrum, it's usually a blind spot for them. The first step is recognizing when there is an opportunity to move toward the middle of the spectrum, and understanding how that could improve your win rate.

INTROVERTS, EXTROVERTS, AND AMBIVERTS

When it comes to Cowboys and Librarians, people are naturally wired toward being one or the other, or somewhere in between. Sometimes people set out to become more aggressive or thoughtful in their approach, but there's a natural point somewhere on the behavioral spectrum that feels most comfortable. This is largely tied to personality. To understand why people approach sales in different ways, it's essential to take a look at personality theories. Popularized by Carl Jung, people started classifying one another and themselves as introverts or extroverts. According to the Merriam Webster Dictionary:

» Extraversion is "the act, state, or habit of being predominantly concerned with obtaining gratification from what is outside the self." Extroverts are energized by social environments and thrive when they are with a group of people.

» Introversion is "the state of or tendency toward being wholly or predominantly concerned with and interested in one's own mental life." Introverts find their energy dwindles during group interaction and they generally prefer to spend time on their own or with a close friend.

If you look at the sales industry as a whole, most salespeople have the reputation for being highly extroverted individuals—smiling, confident, and eager to meet anyone in their path, be it the neighbors, friends of friends, fellow churchgoers, or the person next to them in line at the bank. Natural networkers, extroverts know how to break the ice with a stranger and strike up conversations with people from all walks of life. Instead of worrying about how others will respond, extroverts feel comfortable making small talk, asking questions, or cracking jokes. If the people they talk to are grumpy or don't have much to say, it's no big deal. Most extroverts don't feel like their mood, reputation or self-worth hinges on garnering a positive response in that tiny portion of their day.

An extroverted personality is commonly thought to serve salespeople well, since selling is typically a social role. While the sales experience and level of interaction with customers certainly varies depending on the company and industry, it's hard to sell things to customers without communicating with them. If you're in sales, you probably have to talk to customers in one way or another. Feeling comfortable meeting new people is a basic requirement of being in sales, and nearly all salespeople pass this test.

While society may consider these individuals extroverts, many don't fit this polarizing label. Jung put people into two buckets when examining personality types, but recent research has shown that some people are in the middle of the spectrum as well. Ambiverts are classified as having strong traits of both introverts and extroverts.

Many of the examples I included in this section about feeling comfortable talking to strangers apply to ambiverts as well. For example, when people have something in common, be it a mutual friend or shopping at the same grocery store, it's pretty easy to strike up a conversation related to that commonality. Ambiverts can typically get by in social situations just fine, but that doesn't mean they aren't a little shy in certain environments.

To be honest, I was more of an introvert when I started in sales. I was a shy kid growing up, yet when I got into sales I knew that to be successful I had to get outside of myself. I pretended to be an extrovert, and it brought me out of my shell. (Looking back now makes me realize I probably over compensated in the beginning, which cost me sales. Potential customers probably thought I was too aggressive, just like what I thought about Alex, years later.) After years of being in sales, an unavoidably social role, and gaining maturity, I have become an ambivert.

According to a recent study, my place on the behavioral spectrum has likely contributed to my success.

COWBOYS VS. LIBRARIANS: ROUND 1

Researcher and author Adam Grant from The Warton School conducted a personality survey with more than 300 salespeople to determine where each person fell on the spectrum from extreme extroversion to extreme introversion. He then correlated this data with three months of participants' sales figures. When I heard about this study I was extremely excited to hear about the results! It was the ultimate battle between Cowboys and Librarians! The results would show what I, and so many other salespeople, had been wondering for years. Was it better to approach prospecting with guns blazing, or to do your homework?

Grant found that the most successful salespeople were those who fell somewhere in the middle of the behavioral spectrum. During the study, these ambiverts made 24 percent more than introverts and 32 percent more than extroverts. Most surprising was that salespeople at the far end of the spectrum on both sides made roughly the same sales figures.[21] Have no fear—the tools in the book will help you operate like you're in the middle.

AWARENESS

If you're not closing the majority of your sales then you're missing some because you are relying too much on one side of the Cowboy-Librarian spectrum. Great news though, friends! Increasing your self-awareness can be all you need to start adjusting your approach and improving your win ratio.

Years ago I hired a salesperson for one of my teams and I knew he was a Librarian when it came to his cold calling approach. However, he was very social and friendly so I thought he could interact well with prospects. The challenge was that he was an extreme Librarian, so his interactions with prospects were few and far between. Don't get me wrong, he liked talking to people, but only when he felt well-prepared. I remember one day he spent nine hours putting together a document that would be used to gather information from prospects. The final version was almost identical to the first version, only with a few small changes. He had not realized he spent the whole day on it and accomplished nothing. Certainly not any sales. I sat down with him and explained my observation of his time management for this project, as well as other similar situations where I'd noticed a lot of preparation but not a lot of action. Turns out he had an idea he was over preparing, but he wasn't aware of how extreme his preparation actually had become. For many people, this is a form of call reluctance like we talked about earlier. He was grateful I brought it to his attention, and from that day forward, he became much more conscious of how he spent his time. Today he owns his own company and is still a good friend of mine.

No matter whether you're naturally inclined to act like a Librarian or a Cowboy, when you see the costs and benefits of your behavior, it becomes easier to adjust your approach to get better results.

So how do you know where you fall on the spectrum?

PLAY BOX EXERCISE

Ask three family members, three friends and three clients if they see you as an extrovert or an introvert. You may think you already know what they they'll say, but I encourage you to do this exercise anyway. Many times we see ourselves completely different than others see us. So pick up the phone now and make these calls. You can simply say "Hello ___, I'm working on increasing my sales skills, and I'm reading a book that's taking me through a few exercises. The exercise I'm working on now is about introverts and extroverts, and how other people perceive me. I really value your opinion and am wondering if you can tell me whether you see me as an introvert, or an extrovert?" Tell them you are looking for an honest answer. Then ask them for an example of why they feel that way. For simplicity's sake, don't mention the ambivert.

I did this exercise myself, and the first person I asked was my wife. She said she thought I was somewhere in the middle of being an introvert and an extrovert, which was not a surprise to me. However, what did surprise me was that she said I was more of an extrovert at the office and more of an introvert in our social environment. Honestly, my feelings were a bit hurt! I thought I was always pretty extroverted with our friends, but maybe that shows I have to make a conscious effort to be social in social situations, which does in fact, point to introversion. Although I was a little insulted at first, I know my wife is right. I have both extroverted and introverted tendencies, which make me an ambivert. Being aware of this has actually helped me a lot. Instead of continuing to pretend I'm an extrovert just because I'm in sales and that's what many people think I should be, I can focus on being myself. And as it turns out, my place on the behavioral spectrum is a pretty healthy place for a salesperson to be.

I share this with you because discovering the gaps between how we perceive ourselves and how others perceive us is essential to understanding what's stopping us from being more successful in sales. Now that you have a better idea of how others perceive you, it will be easier to understand how to grow as a salesperson and an individual.

ADAPT TO THE PROSPECT

We've talked about mirroring and matching prospects, and it's important to think about that from the Cowboy/Librarian perspective as well. To connect with prospects, you need to be on their level and relate with them. If you are hardwired as a Cowboy, you might naturally connect best with High Ds. If you are hardwired as a Librarian, you might best relate to High Cs. As you look back on the successful sales relationships you've built with prospects and customers, you can probably tell the types of personality/behavior that you mesh with well. Having this awareness will help you realize when you need to work harder to adapt to other types, and show how although it may feel a little uncomfortable to you, it will be appreciated by your prospects. Tuning in and truly listening to prospects over the phone will help you know if you need to turn your Cowboy or Librarian tendencies down or up a notch.

SUMMARY

As a rule in life, balance will usually serve you well. When you are on the far end of anything, be it an approach, school of thought, or stance on a particular topic, the harder it's going to be for you to relate to certain people who don't share your viewpoints. Since sales is about connecting with others, it's important to take a balanced approach to prospecting. You don't want to be too aggressive or not aggressive enough. It can sometimes be tricky to figure out where that line stands, but it helps to know it's there, and understand whether you tend to fall on a certain side.

KEY TAKEAWAYS

» Have self-awareness: Determine whether you're a natural Cowboy or Librarian

» Work on balance: You'll be most successful with a balanced approach

» Adapt to prospects: Pay attention and know when you can push harder toward one end of the spectrum

CHAPTER 10

· · · · · · · · · ·

THE FORTUNE IS IN THE FOLLOW UP

"Persist and persevere, and you will find most things that are attainable, possible."

Philip Stanhope, 4th Earl of Chesterfield

You know that feeling when you contact a new prospect for the first time and you easily close him or her on the spot? The stars align perfectly in that best-case-scenario moment and you just can't believe your good fortune. Depending on what you sell, this may happen occasionally or never happen at all. But if your prospects haven't already been vetted, I'd be willing to bet that it doesn't happen very often.

Most people need at least a little bit of time before they are ready to make a purchase. That's why the majority of sales come from following up with prospects. From my experience, about 70 percent of my clients have always come from follow up. Sometimes it only takes one follow-up touch point to close them, and other times it takes many. Sometimes prospects seem ready to buy but they never do, and other times they are ready to sign much quicker than originally expected. The follow-up process can seem frustratingly illusive, especially if you're newer to sales, but getting good at it is essential to being a top salesperson.

There's an art to effective follow up that gets real results. Instead of thinking of it as a challenge, I like to think of it as an opportunity to excel. I've built my business on mastering the follow-up process, and I know I wouldn't be where I am today without it. In this chapter, we'll cover what you need to know to become a master at follow up and take your career to the next level.

THE DUAL APPROACH: CLOSING AND BUILDING YOUR BRAND

During the follow-up process, it's easy to focus on getting the sale and doing it as quickly as possible. Closing is great, but you need to realize that some prospects just aren't ready to buy today and they won't be ready to buy anytime soon. But that doesn't mean they'll never buy from you. The trick is building your brand through follow-up communication so that six months, one year, or even 10 years later when prospects are finally ready to buy, they think of you personally, and of your company. Each phone call, email, or direct mail piece they receive can get you a little bit closer to closing the deal. I want to be clear that follow up is not just systems, emails, phone calls, and touch points; it's a mindset. And every touch point is forward progress. It can be easy to get frustrated when you follow up with leads and they don't bite. You might start to feel like your efforts are a waste of time, but trust me, they aren't. When you connect with customers, you're also doing some marketing for your own personal brand and your company.

Garrett Lenderman of KW Publishing said that staying top of mind with potential clients the name of the game.[22] If you're top of mind, when prospects make a decision or come to a realization that they need a product or service like the one you offer, you're there to make a sale. That will most commonly come down to the amount of times you reach out to someone. The quality adds to the effectiveness of your offerings.

I love using the phone for follow up because it's personal and it leaves a stronger memory than other communication methods. When people hear my voice and listen to me say my name and my company's name, it's embedded into their minds a little deeper. Even if they aren't in the market for my services today, a year from now when they are, they'll think of me. I've had it happen over and over. People don't always remember my company name, but they remember me. That's why it's so important to make the follow-up process personal and continue connecting with prospects on a deeper level.

KNOW THE DECISION-MAKERS

How do your prospects make purchasing decisions? Is it up to one person or a team of people? Does a certain person handle all of the research and vetting, and get another person to sign off on it? Companies and individuals make decisions in a variety of ways, and interpersonal dynamics often plays a role. The decision-making process can be unclear for salespeople, in both B to B and B to C. That's why a big part of our job is figuring out who has the authority to buy what we're selling. Without knowing that, our efforts can easily be misguided.

The earlier in the sales cycle you can determine the real decision maker, the better, but I've found that it often comes up in follow up. If you were talking to the decision maker the first time you called, there's a greater chance you would have gotten a straight yes or no answer because that person is empowered to decide. People who aren't empowered to make decisions on their own tend to go with "maybe" answers that warrant follow up. Of course not all maybes come from non-decision makers, but it should raise a flag that you need to confirm the decision-making process.

The easiest way to understand who makes decisions is to ask. But you need to be careful here so that you don't come off as offensive. Step up the friendliness in your tone of voice and set up the question so it doesn't feel like it comes out of left field. For example, if you're trying to sell patio furniture to a woman, don't say: "Are you allowed to buy things without your husband's approval?" I guarantee that will not go well! Instead, try something like: "I want to make the decision-making process as easy as possible for you, and provide the right information to everyone. Should we be involving any other family members in our discussions?... OK, great. I just want to make sure we aren't leaving anyone out." You can easily adapt this script for B to B as well. This can be a delicate question and feel a little awkward at first, so make sure you practice it through role-playing. Many times the best solution is to simply ask, "Are you the final decision maker?" Most people will respect you not wasting their time and tell you.

GATEKEEPERS

It may feel like gatekeepers block you from your decision maker, but sometimes they *are* your decision maker. In order to properly direct your follow-up efforts, it's important to differentiate between the makers and fakers. The higher up you go in a company, the more people rely on support from colleagues for vetting vendors. Someone at the C-Suite or VP level might need to sign off on major purchases, but they often defer to their administrative assistant or a director. If you're in contact with someone who reports information to the decision maker, don't dismiss that person as unimportant. It's essential to get him or her on your side, either to give you access to the real decision maker or to tell the decision maker to hire you. You should ask gatekeepers about how decisions are made, using the same strategy I just described. If you are polite and respectful, saying that you want to make yourself available to answer questions from all stakeholders, you shouldn't worry about offending anyone. Remember when we talked about the DISC, the higher up the chain you go, the more likely the decision maker and their gatekeeper will operate in the High D realm and will appreciate directness.

GO FOR THE EMAIL

Making follow-up calls is a great way to connect with prospects and build your personal brand, but it is a labor-intensive process, especially when you have a lot of calls to make. Automating follow up through email is a smart option to ensure you stay in touch with prospects who aren't ready to buy anytime soon. Obviously, the first step here is getting the prospect's email address if you don't have it already.

I often find that the best approach to getting an email address is to be casual about it and assume prospects will give it to you. You want to be polite, but you can frame it in a way where it doesn't sound like you're asking for permission, which could trigger the reaction that they might want to think about it and say no. Instead, think of getting their email as a quick and easy necessary step in being able to help them later. Here's an example: "I understand your contract doesn't end until April. That's actually great timing for switching vendors, since we usually run special discounts in the spring. I'll take down your email to make sure you get included in those promotions." Or you can simply ask, "What's the best email address?" and wait for the answer. You would be surprised at how many people pause and give it to you.

Sometimes prospects will try to give you a generic or shared email account, such as "info@___." This type of address is much less valuable than a personal email address. Sales messages that aren't directed to an individual seem like junk and will be deleted or ignored. In fact, if you use an email marketing platform to send your emails, many companies prohibit adding that kind of address to your database because of spam laws. When prospects give you a generic email address, explain how it's actually better for them to receive your emails directly. You can also say that unfortunately your system won't allow you to enter that kind of email address, but you want to make sure they receive those special offers. When prospects are reluctant to give me an email, I always remind them that they can easily opt out with one click at any time if they do not find our information helpful. Most people are ok with that because, like me, they probably opt out of email campaigns regularly and know how easy it is.

Once you have prospects' email addresses, it becomes much easier to communicate with them on an ongoing long-term basis and follow the important rule: Never Close a Contact. Whether you send e-blasts through an email marketing platform, your marketing team does it for you, or you send regular emails using the BCC function, everyone in your database should be receiving ongoing email communication from you. Considering how easy it is to send email campaigns nowadays, this should be a given. (In fact, ongoing email communication should be the bare minimum of follow up.) Don't let your database sit without any type of communication scheduled. The only exception to this is if you do regular mailings to the prospect and do not have an email address.

A best practice is to divide your contact list into segments based on different criteria so that you can better tailor your email marketing. You can create segments based on warm or cold leads, type of product or service the prospect is most interested in, clients vs. non-clients, geographic location, and many other differentiators. In real estate, we find it most helpful to categorize by A, B or C, clients. If you use a CRM system or email marketing platform, it's easy to upload contacts, even if you want to include them in multiple lists. From there, you can send automated e-blasts, also known as drip campaigns. Prospects can get a certain e-blast one month after you add them to your database, a different e-blast another month later, and so on. You can also send the same e-blasts to everyone at once, which is helpful for special sales and holidays. All e-blasts should include your name and contact information or look like it's coming from your email account, so the business comes back to you if/when it converts.

I've had an email marketing system in place for a long time and it makes my job so much easier. Younger salespeople might take email marketing for granted because they've always had it as a tool, but it's really changed what's possible in sales. Even though I have the most success selling on the phone, supplementing my efforts with e-blasts is a key part of my sales playbook. It can take prospects multiple times of hearing my name and my company's name before they become familiar with what I can offer and motivated to work with me. Automated e-blasts help with those touch points so when I make a follow-up call, prospects are further along in the sales cycle, and they recognize me. It's amazing how many compliments I get from people I do not do business with yet, who say, "Wow you guys do a great job marketing!"

TAILOR YOUR APPROACH

In a previous chapter, we talked about the importance of observing your prospects' behavior type and tailoring your communication style to match. In the follow-up process, this is even more important because you get to know prospects a little better and it takes finesse to successfully build those relationships. If you took great notes the first time you spoke with a prospect, you should know what approach you're going to take before you make the follow-up call. If the prospect is a High D, you know you'll need to be direct and respect their time. With a High I, you'll need to keep building those social connections and making small talk. With a High C, you'll focus on proactively providing information to help with their decision. With a High S, you'll focus on building relationships, but in the context of helping them get the results they're after. You want to home in on how your prospects are wired and match your approach to their preferences.

In addition to adjusting your communication to prospects' behavioral style, it's important to cater to their logistical preferences as well. Just like the message in your sales presentation, the sales process should be all about the client. If you typically like doing business over the phone but your prospect suggests a video chat, you should agree that's a great idea and figure out how to make it work. (It doesn't matter if you hate the idea. It isn't about you. If you want to meet in person but that isn't convenient for your prospect, you should find another option that works for both of you. The key is to be flexible and understand that not everyone works the same way you do. You will have much better outcomes by adjusting your normal approach to make prospects comfortable. This will show you are willing to go out of your way to provide great service and support, which is something clients are always looking for, no matter what you sell. A lot of companies are catching on to this concept and describing it as "meeting clients where they are." (If you're nervous about closing through a different medium such as video, ask someone to partner with you to help you feel more comfortable. You need to be flexible, but being ill-prepared or nervous won't serve you well.)

My friend Amelia just had an experience that shows what happens when salespeople are unwilling to adjust their approach. She won a free two-week trial membership to a new gym. It sounded great, but the gym was all the way across town. A salesperson called her soon after to follow up, saying the offer was only good for a couple of weeks, so she would have to act fast. Amelia was going on vacation soon and didn't want to start the trial yet, but she said she would be happy to sign the agreement in advance. The salesperson said that was fine, and pushed to set up an in-person meeting at the gym. Amelia said she preferred not to come all the way to the other side of town if she wasn't going to work out that day, and she asked the salesperson to email her the contract to sign and return. The salesperson said they don't really send things via email. Instead, she kept pushing for Amelia to come in. Amelia said she would consider it, but that she was really busy. The salesperson called back a couple of days later and they had almost the exact same conversation again. She pushed for the in-person meeting at the gym and my friend didn't bite.

Over the next couple of weeks, the salesperson called back eight times and left two voicemails. Amelia actually had been excited about winning the free gym membership and fully intended on giving the gym a try, but the salesperson blew it. Instead of making the experience pleasant and easy for the customer by catering to her preferences, the salesperson tried to force the customer into doing business a different way. And it didn't work. No one wants to keep having the same conversation over and over, with one person trying to wear the other down. The salesperson was so set on the idea that she had to meet prospects at the gym that she was unable to solve an easy logistical problem. Remember, my friend never had an issue with accepting the free trial membership, signing the paperwork, or meeting in person; she just didn't want to go all the way across town to do it. The salesperson could have asked if another location or neighborhood was more convenient. If Amelia still refused to meet in person, it would have shown that convenience wasn't the real issue, and that she wasn't really interested. In that case, the salesperson would have known to move on. However, if Amelia was happy to meet in a more convenient location, the salesperson would have gotten the paperwork signed and advanced the relationship. She could have also taken the opportunity to talk up the gym's neighborhood, making the location seem like a positive, despite the commute.

Whatever the reasoning behind the salesperson's actions, she missed important cues that cost the sale. A one-size-fits-all approach just doesn't work for everyone. To better understand why the approach didn't work in this particular situation, let's consider my friend's personality. She has taken the DISC assessment, and she's a High I with High D as a close second. In this case, the High D was easy to see. Time and efficiency are important to her and she was direct in telling the salesperson how she preferred to receive information. The High I might have been harder to identify early on, but showed in her behavior of ignoring all of the follow-up calls. High Is value positive relationships, so it's easy to see how a salesperson's inflexibility or unwillingness to accommodate would be enough to bring this relationship to a screeching halt. Alternately, if the salesperson made the effort to meet in a convenient location, it would have done a lot to build the relationship and likely lead to a loyal client.

As you do your follow up calls, don't let yourself go on autopilot. Each call will be different and you will need to respond in different ways. If you lump all follow-up calls into one group in your mind, your communication will suffer and you won't be as effective or creative. And you won't be able to meet clients where they are, either literally or figuratively. When you start to find yourself losing steam after making a lot of follow-up calls, take a break and do something else for a while. Follow up can be hard work, and it's essential that you're mentally present on your calls so you can make it all about the client.

Years ago a sales guru told me, "If you're not in the right mindset and you can't get in the right mindset, then skip the calls and come back to them when you are in the right mindset." I agree with this and would prefer to skip a call session because I am off that day rather than risk jeopardizing a relationship.

FOLLOW UP TIPS:

There are a variety of simple ways to improve your follow up efforts. Keep the following tips in mind when you're making calls.

Come from contribution: Prospects will respond more favorably to your follow-up efforts if you show you are trying to help them. You can do this in a variety of ways, but one of the best is to offer something valuable. This can be a free consultation, a free informational piece, or a monetary offer, such as a discount. People aren't dumb—they know you are trying to make a sale. But they respect when you make it a win-win and offer something valuable to them. This also helps you to avoid coming across as pushy. Even when prospects aren't interested in buying at the time, they are more likely to remember you in a positive way if you have come from a point of contribution.

Leave good voicemails: It's helpful for prospects to know you've called (and it serves as a touch point), but you don't want to leave so much information on their voicemail that there's no reason for them to call you back. The goal is to have a live conversation, so you want to leave just enough information to pique their interest. If you've talked to them before, refer back to your notes on their DISC behavior type, and think about the type of voicemail that would resonate best. If you think you'll have a better chance of a prospect texting you back than calling you back, go ahead and invite him or her to do so when you leave the voicemail. That will at least keep the conversation going until you can talk live. (Personally, I am a fan of keeping voicemails as short sale possible and always leave something of value.)

Mix it up: Many people have daily routines where certain times of the day or certain days just don't work for phone calls. If you've only tried calling in the morning, try the afternoon. If you called on Thursday last week, choose a different day this week. If you're still having trouble getting your prospect to answer the phone, try calling from a different line. I'm not telling you to be shady and use a payphone or a friend's phone, but it helps to have a separate cell and office line. I have five different phone numbers I can call from. I track the times and phone numbers I use in follow up so I can try different combinations. This is obviously more useful if you're working on getting an A prospect on the phone than a regular follow-up call with a C prospect.

Use a dialer system: This is a great system for making a lot of calls and leaving a lot of voicemails efficiently. You can load a list of phone numbers into a dialer system, and the system will call one number after the other. When someone picks up, you are connected to the call. Otherwise, the dialer automatically leaves a pre-recorded voicemail at the same time it calls the next number. The voicemail is general, but it can work for a variety of situations. My recorded message says something like, "Hi, this is David Hill at Hill Team Associates. I am following up on our conversation. Please call me back when you get a chance. My number is ___." Simple and direct.

Supplement direct mail and email with calls: Every time you mail something to a prospect, it gives you a good reason to call. If you sent something useful, like a marketing piece, a promo, or even a notepad or desk calendar, you're likely to find prospects friendlier when you call to check whether they received it. Direct mail is expensive, so you only want to include warm and fresh leads in your efforts. Creativity counts here because you want to stand out and get noticed. Just make sure you don't send out more direct mail than you can keep up with in your calls. The same strategy works for supplementing emails with calls. After I email information to a prospect, I like to follow up with a quick call, leaving a voicemail if no one picks up. I'll say something like, "I just sent you an email. Take a look when you get a chance." This helps ensure my email doesn't get overlooked and reinforces the fact that I am expecting the prospect to respond.

A holiday strategy: I've experienced great results following up with prospects around the holidays, and I always share my strategy with the salespeople I coach. The strategy is to make three touch points within a short period of time: a call to wish prospects a happy holiday season, a (non-religious) holiday card, and another call to wish prospects a happy new year. I found this is a great strategy because you're up against less competition. Most salespeople go on autopilot around the holidays and pull back on their follow up efforts, thinking prospects will be too busy to consider buying anything that isn't a holiday gift. But the buyers at this time of year can actually be very serious. Many of my coaching clients get immediate sales from this strategy and also fill the pipeline with spring and summer business.

Get executives to pick up: Sometimes gatekeepers won't give you access to the senior executive who makes decisions. For B to B sales, a great tip is to call the main line early in the morning before normal work hours. Senior staff members typically arrive to the office before other employees and they are motivated to pick up the phone if the administrator isn't in yet.

Be smart about timing: Sometimes prospects say they need to discuss things with their colleagues before making a hiring decision. You always want to ask for the timeline when they expect the discussion to take place. Sometimes the prospect will tell you that their next meeting is scheduled on X date, and they'll follow up with you after that. When that happens, I would normally ask the prospect to let me know if he or she needs any additional information in the meantime. But instead of waiting until after the meeting, I would generally check back in a couple of days before, just to offer any additional help preparing materials or information. This shows I am organized and proactively offer support, which leaves a good impression right before they make a decision.

Don't ignore stalls: Sometimes prospects will tell you they expect to make a decision by a certain date, but that date comes and goes without any progress. It's hard to know if they are still interested and encountered a genuine setback, or if they just don't feel comfortable telling you they are no longer interested. As you learned earlier in this book, you have a lot to gain by playing to win and shouldn't be afraid of getting shot down. The best way to gauge interest is to be direct. You should say something like, "Hey, I know you said you were going to get back to me with a decision by X day. Are you still interested? Did something come up?" You want to get a real answer, even if you don't think it's the answer you want to hear. When prospects tell you they aren't interested, you can at least be sure you aren't wasting your time. Many prospects will appreciate your offer for them to be direct.

Ask for help: If you don't have enough bandwidth to make all of your follow-up calls in a timely manner, ask for help. Many sales organizations have roles where people are solely in charge of follow-up calls. In other organizations, administrative assistants can pitch in and help when the sales team is slammed, like right after a tradeshow. If you explain to prospects upfront that you work as a team with your colleagues, it will be OK if someone else helps with your follow-up calls. My company has used a service called Upwork to find freelancers to help us when we get extra busy. This type of service is typically quicker and less expensive than going through a recruiter or posting a job only and vetting candidates.

WHEN TO STOP CALLING

We talked about the importance of prequalifying leads in Chapter 5— Play to Win vs. Playing Not to Lose, but after your initial prequalification, things are going to change. Prospects will either keep moving forward in the sales cycle or the opportunity could cool down and seem less likely to close. Make sure you pay attention to what's changing and adjust your approach accordingly.

I've seen salespeople call the same prospects over and over again every few months for years. Well, not only have I seen it, I've done it.

And I'm here to tell you not to do it! It will drag you down and suck your energy. Every time you see certain prospects' names come up on your follow-up reminder, you'll dread calling them. And coming from a place of dread isn't a good approach to sales or healthy for maintaining your positive mindset. If you have ever looked at a follow up call and thought to yourself, "oh this one again," that may be a sign. (Just sayin'!)

Additionally, it's safe to say that once you call people several times and leave messages, it's not an accident if they never call you back. They aren't interested. It's very easy to block numbers on cell phones today, and you don't want prospects to block you. There's a line between being persistent and harassing or stalking someone, so make sure you don't cross it. Depending on what you sell, there might be a different standard for when to stop calling prospects. I've heard that five unreturned calls is a good number to go by. Whatever you think is best for your industry, keep in mind that you only have so much time in your day. When you stop calling dead leads, you'll have more time to focus on fresh ones.

If you have the contact's email list, you can keep sending automated emails since you Never Close a Contact. However, if you don't have the email address, you'll need to decide when you're finished trying to contact them. I recommend the following Play Call: **the last message message.** This is a voicemail where you clearly explain that this will be the very last time you call them. When I leave this message, I like to remind prospects of some type of offer, and repeat this is my last time calling them. I put a reminder in my calendar for two weeks out, and if the prospect hasn't called me back by then, I delete the contact info from the system. About 10 percent of the time, prospects do call me back. I guess it goes to show that people suddenly want what they think they might not be able to get.

Sometimes sales organizations don't like deleting contact information, even if it's incomplete or the prospects haven't shown interest. In some cases, it can be valuable to hold onto this info and check back at a much later date. As an example, I just had a call reminder come up that I set 21 months ago. It was a cancelled seller who was about to hang up on me and told me he was renting the house and not to call him again. Before he hung up I asked him how long he rented it for. He said two years then click. I could have deleted him from the system, but I thought what the heck, I'll try him again in about two years. When I called back he had no idea who I was, but as a matter of fact, he was interested in selling and said he would love to meet in person. As you can see, the fortune truly is in the follow up.

SUMMARY

Since the majority of sales come from follow up, it's usually one of the skills salespeople can work on that will make the biggest impact. There's a difference between going through the motions and doing it right. If you take the time to master follow up, I guarantee it'll make a huge difference in your results.

KEY TAKEAWAYS

» Tailor your approach: One size doesn't fit all

» Go for the email: Automate follow up and Never Close a Contact

» Play to win: A quick no is better than a long waste of time no

» 70% of business comes from follow up in most industries

CHAPTER 11

· · · · · · · · · ·

BEYOND THE PLAYBOOK

"Everyone communicates, few connect."

John Maxwell

We've covered a lot of information so far in *The Sales Playbook* and we're reaching the end of our journey together. But that doesn't mean you can put this book on your shelf and forget about it. You can collect thousands of books and have the smartest bookshelf in the world, but if you don't take the time to truly absorb the information, learn it, and use it to take action in your life, what use is it? Probably not much. Applying what you read will be the difference between getting the results you want and having everything stay the same. It's hard work to go beyond reading good advice, but it's worth it. Trust me! You've gotten this far, and you're well on your way to taking your career to the next level. In this chapter, I share some final thoughts to help you move beyond the playbook.

NURTURE YOUR MINDSET

Many people go into sales because they think it's easy and flexible. They want to come and go and make their own schedule. But pretty soon they realize that sales is hard work. Really hard work! Working in sales has the potential to get people down mentally more than a lot of other professions. That's why it's essential to nurture a positive mindset on an ongoing basis.

You work hard at overcoming rejection when you are new to sales, but your efforts can't stop there. You must always be aware of your mental state and how interactions affect it. When you are having a tough day, ask yourself why you are really in sales. Thinking back to your Big Why, maybe it's to challenge yourself and see what you're capable of, or support your family, or help individuals or businesses improve the way they do something. Whatever your Big Why, when you're doing something for the right purposes you'll be able to keep doing it.

Sometimes people quit sales because they get too stressed and discouraged. It's a head game. You have to know that no matter how good your skills are you won't get them all. Ever.

Salespeople often hire me to help them take their performance to the next level, and the first thing we typically work on is figuring out a way to have fun while making calls. Being in a good mood can change everything, especially effectiveness and performance. I always advise salespeople not to take themselves too seriously. It helps to lighten up a bit and see each call for what it is—just one small part of their day, and a tiny part of their career. When salespeople get too wrapped up thinking each call is extremely important, they get stuck in their heads worrying about performing to the best of their abilities, instead of simply being present on the call.

Several years ago, I had the opportunity to audition for a pretty huge speaking engagement. I knew the audition was coming for months and I had practiced my presentation over and over. I knew the whole script by heart and even presented it three times in my office and got great feedback. But when I showed up for the audition there were three very high level people in the room who intimidated me. I didn't expect them and they threw me off my game. The audition went terribly. I was so worried about my performance that I couldn't focus on doing my presentation. I even forgot most of my scripts. I got evaluations of my performance and the feedback wasn't surprising. I was told that I did not smile at all or look happy to be there. One of the evaluations simply said that I needed to get out of my head.

I did not get the gig, but I learned a very important lesson that day: I should do my best to prepare, but relax after I put in the work. By worrying about my performance, I wasn't enabling myself to smile and have fun, which are two things I needed to do to have a great performance. Obviously, I wasn't doing myself any favors by worrying. Having this experience was necessary for me to learn this lesson and move to the next level. I read somewhere that "you're either failing or you're learning." To me, this was a failing experience that lead to a learning experience.

Hopefully my story will help you skip the failing part and go straight to the learning part! You should take a step back and put things in perspective before you make sales calls. When you think about it, what is the worst that can happen? Will you be arrested or have to go to the hospital over a botched call? Well I guess in the ultimate extreme that could happen but for the other 99.999 percent of the time the answer is NO! The only thing that can really be injured is your ego. So really who cares if people say no? What do you have to lose? You never had that prospect's business in the first place so the worst case is that things will stay the same. You break even! You have to be OK with NO!

DON'T LOSE FAITH IN THE PHONE

Mastering phone prospecting will open the door for what you've been wanting most out of your job. Whether your goal is to make more money, have better job security, improve your work/life balance, or simply find your job more fulfilling, all of these outcomes are a result of becoming more effective. It's hard work to master your skills on the phone, but I promise you it's worth it.

When you feel confident on the phone, you are empowered to make the best communication choices available to you and take a more strategic approach to your job. Instead of leaning on email like a crutch, you will know when to pick up the phone and how to guide meaningful conversations that drive results. You will go from a reactive approach to a proactive approach, gaining more control over your schedule and outcomes. You will experience what it's like to better connect with prospects, which will remind you of why you decided to go into sales in the first place. When you spend every single day doing what you love about sales—whether it's meeting new people, helping them solve challenges, winning them over, or challenging yourself—it will make your career always feel exciting and new.

To get these outcomes and more, you have to commit to practicing, learning, and mastering the information we've covered in this book. Effort and hard work will get you there. Here's a recap of the key takeaways from each chapter.

Chapter 1: Getting Smart with the Phone

Using the phone to talk with prospects will help you:

» Be more strategic: Learn more about prospects and better tailor your communication

» Increase productivity: Know which leads to pursue and manage your time better

» Reinforce why you went into sales: Helping more people and closing more deals feels good

Chapter 2: Connect or Be Disconnected

» Master your first impression: The first seven seconds are crucial

» Mirror and match prospects: Pace, mood, and language

» Identify personality types: Tailor your presentation to the prospect's personality

Chapter 3: Lifting the 800 lb. Phone

» Mindset: Your thoughts become your reality. You are in control of your thoughts.

» Numbers: You won't win them all and you don't need to.

» Contribute: Your job is to provide information that helps people make their own decisions.

Chapter 4: Get Systematized or Get Lost

» Write everything down.

» Schedule follow-up call reminders for specific dates.

» Protect your "free" time with time blocking.

Chapter 5: Playing to Win vs. Playing Not to Lose

» Go after the best opportunities: Prequalify to prioritize

» Don't get used: Track the time you spend helping prospects and clients for free

» Talk pricing: Get on the same page with prospects to ensure you aren't wasting each other's time

Chapter 6: The Road to Mastery

» Practice Deliberately: Follow the four components

» Use Scripts: Memorize, Internalize, Customize (In that order!)

» Role-Play: The most effective way to practice

Chapter 7: The Customer Experience Revolution

» Develop a communication system: Know how often you should contact customers

» Track your outreach: it should be easy to reference your interactions with customers

» Cater to customers: make interactions about them, not you

» Get reviews and testimonials

Chapter 8: Stop Telling and Start Listening

» Use the 70/30 Rule: Listen 70 percent of the time and talk 30 percent of the time

» The Benefit AND: Remember your prospect is thinking, "So what? Who cares? What about me?"

» Be present in your conversations: Listening is different from not talking

Chapter 9: Cowboys and Librarians

» Have self-awareness: Determine whether you're a natural Cowboy or Librarian

» Work on balance: You'll be most successful with a balanced approach

» Adapt to prospects: Pay attention and know when you can push harder toward one end of the spectrum

Chapter 10: The Fortune is in the Follow Up

» Tailor your approach: One size doesn't fit all

» Go for the email: Automate follow up and Never Close a Contact

» Play to win: A quick no is better than a long waste of time no

» 70 percent of business comes from follow up in most industries

FINAL THOUGHT AND FINAL PLAY CALL

You know how you feel when you make the last call of the day? You hang up and think, "Ok, that's it, I'm done!" But if you decide to pick up the phone one more time, that is always the call that turns into gold. This has happened for me dozens of times in my career. I was about to give up but decided to make that one extra call and that is where I found my reward. I encourage you to do the same thing. Make that one extra call, practice that one extra script, and when someone says no, ask that one extra time. The extra one is where you will find your success.

CITATIONS

· · · · · · · · · ·

ENDNOTES

1. "Seven Seconds to Make a First Impression," *Forbes.com,* February 13, 2011, http://www.forbes.com/sites/carolkinseygoman/2011/02/13/seven-seconds-to-make-a-first-impression/.

2. Tero Kuttinen, "Typical American without a landline: A 27-year old Latino living in Columbus, Ohio," *BGR*, PUBLICATION DATE AND/OR ACCESS DATE, http://bgr.com/2013/01/02/us-landline-usage-study-2012-279607/.

3. David Mamet, *Glengarry Glen Ross*, film, directed by James Foley (1992; Los Angeles: New Line Cinema).

4. John Alexandrov, interview by David Hill, Date June 2015.

5. Jairek Robbins, *Live It!: Achieve Success by Living with Purpose* (Grand Haven, MI: Grand Harbor Press, 2014), 62–70.

6. Anthony Robbins and Joseph McClendon, *Unlimited Power: A Black Choice* (New York: Simon & Schuster, 1997), 361–2.

7. Jessie, interview by author, October 2, 2015.

8. Gary Keller, interview by author, July 16, 2015.

9. Ana Dutra, *Leadershit*, Hogan. (To be published 2016.)

10. Ashley, interview by Amelia Forczak, August 19, 2015.

11. Michael Phelps and Alan Abrahamson, *No Limits: The Will to Succeed* (New York: Free Press, 2008), 151.

12. Craig Lord, "Franklin Pips Phelps For Top Honour," *SwimNews.com,* Sept 16, 2012, http://www.swimnews.com/News/view/9743.

13. K. Anders Ericsson, Ralf Th. Krampe, and Clemens Tesch-Romer, "The Role of Deliberate Practice in the Acquisition of Expert Performance," *Psychological Review* 100, no. 3 (1993): 363–406.

14. James Clear, "Lessons on Success and Deliberate Practice from Mozart, Picasso, and Kobe Bryant," *JamesClear.com,* accessed October 14, 2015, http://jamesclear.com/deliberate-practice.

15. Kyle Buchanan, "Anthony Hopkins: The Movieline Interview," *Movieline,* April 12, 2010, http://movieline.com/2010/04/12/anthony-hopkins-the-movieline-interview/.

16. Jake Sorofman, "Gartner Surveys Confirm Customer Experience Is the New Battlefield," *Gartner,* October 23, 2014, http://blogs.gartner.com/jake-sorofman/gartner-surveys-confirm-customer-experience-new-battlefield/.

17. Flannery, interview by author, October 1, 2015.

18. Kevin Sheridan, interview by author, October 6, 2015.

19. Zig Ziglar, "Official Ziglar Quotes," *Ziglar.com,* accessed November 20, 2015, http://www.ziglar.com/quotes/you-can-have-everything-life-you-want.

20. Darren Hardy, *The Entrepreneur Roller Coaster: Why Now Is the Time to #JoinTheRide* (Lake Dallas, TX: Success, 2015), PAGE #S.

21. David DiSalvo, "Move Over Extroverts, Here Come the Ambiverts," *Forbes.com,* April 10, 2013, http://www.forbes.com/sites/daviddisalvo/2013/04/10/move-over-extroverts-here-come-the-ambiverts/

22. Garrett Lenderman, email message to author, December 8, 2015.

ACKNOWLEDGEMENTS

· · · · · · · · · ·

First and foremost, I have to acknowledge my excellent and beautiful wife Vee. Without her continuing to push me and tell me I can do it, tell me to keep going despite the ups and downs, and tell me that my book will be super successful, I am certain I would not have finished writing. Vee was the inspiration that kept me going mentally throughout this long process.

I also want to thank Gary Keller, John Alexandrov, John Chapin and the others who let me pick their brains, which made a great contribution to the book.

I want to thank Amelia Forczak, who ghostwrote the book with me. Amelia was the technical inspiration that kept me moving forward. She was able to take everything from my head and articulate it perfectly on paper. Every time I read her edits it got me excited and made it so much easier to keep moving forward. Thank you, Amelia!

I also want to personally thank you for picking up *The Sales Playbook*. Without you buying it, this book does not exist. I hope you love it, share it, and use it as a tool to prosper on your journey to sales mastery.

Last but not least, I have to thank the three people who could have discouraged me from writing this book. When I excitedly told them my plans, they looked at me like I was crazy. One person even said, "Wow, really, you?" (Not in a positive way.) I responded that I have been on the phone more than 28 years and wanted to help others with what I had learned along the way. They doubtfully replied, "hmm" and changed the subject. Thanks to all three of you for inspiring me greatly. I wish you could see the smile on my face right now.

CPSIA information can be obtained
at www.ICGtesting.com
Printed in the USA
BVOW08s1009280717
490081BV00006B/16/P